Plannin
Architect
urban
Social +

1st ed - wrps

957

5134191693
266-4

PLAYING URBAN GAMES

PLAYING URBAN GAMES
the systems approach to planning

by martin kuenzlen
with the collaboration of tyrone cashman & hartmut happ

*Acknowledgements to all persons who
supported me in all my difficulties during the
process of writing this book, especially to*

Naomi Lev
Tom and Mary McNulty
Claus Offe
Robbie Pfeufer
Judy Schwartz
Alex Tzonis

i press incorporated
145 Hanover Street
Boston, Mass. 02108

Distributed by George Braziller Inc.
One Park Avenue
New York, N. Y. 10016

Library of Congress Catalog Card Number: 75-189032
First Printing
Printed in the United States of America

FOREWORD

It is the essence of capitalism that both goods and labor power are typically bought and sold on the market. In such a society relations among individuals are dominated by the principle of the exchange, of QUID PRO QUO, not only in economic matters but in all other aspects of life as well . . . such central category of bourgeois thought is but one symptom of the profoundly contradictory nature of monopoly capitalism, of the ever-sharpening conflict between the rapidly advancing rationalization of the actual process of production and the undiminished *elementality* of the system as a whole. This conflict affects all aspects of society.

— BARAN AND SWEEZY IN *MONOPOLY CAPITAL*

Contents

INTRODUCTION

The sense of impending doom in American cities grows as each year passes. Every American city dweller is inexorably confronted with massive unsolved problems, leaving him with the feeling of living at the base of a volcano. Some consider the growing chaos as "characteristic" and inevitable, some feel that it results from the rapid development of industrial technology, or that it is caused by uncontrolled migration, some find its source in the general population explosion, and some believe the cause to be lack of money and of practical political strategies.

Not one but all of these factors point only to the surface of the problem. The decline of the cities derives not from technical problems but from the antagonistic contradictions within the structure of the society itself.

This structure in its final results produces contradictions like those in feudal times where a few kings and lords used their political and economic power to make people dependent on them and to exploit and oppress land, people, villages and towns. Their castles and palaces — the environmental structure reflects distinctly a social structure built on privileges for the powerholders and the oppression of the people dependent on them.

In like manner our present cities reflect the capitalists' power and domination over people. The cities have become "capitalist castles" and instruments to subordinate, exploit and exhaust the people. This system of exploitation causes many of the downtrodden to attempt to "make it big" to escape from the morass themselves, thereby oppressing others, thus turning the cities into scenes of *urban massacres* — the execution of hopes and loves and the completion of alienation and repression.

Planners involved in *systems* and *social research,* now believe they can, with their new technocratic methods, save the cities from further decay and dissolution. Their approach, however, though drawing enormous attention, is highly questionable. This is the subject of a critical analysis within the following chapters.

PLAYING URBAN GAMES

Greek οὐ not + τόπος place ; see -IA ¹.]   **1.** An imaginary island, depicted by Sir Thomas More as enjoying a perfect social, legal, and political system. **b.** *transf.* Any imaginary or indefinitely-remote region, country, or locality 1610.   **2.** A place, state, or condition ideally perfect in respect of politics, laws, customs, and conditions 1613.   **b.** An impossibly ideal scheme, esp. for social improvement 1734.

1. b. Ignorant where this River rises,..whether in Asia, in Africa, or in U. 1684.   **2. b.** Averse to all enthusiasm, mysticism, utopias, and superstition LECKY.

Utopian (yutōu·piăn), *a.* and *sb.* 1551. [ad. mod.L. *Utopianus* ; see prec. and -AN.]   **A.** *adj.* **1.** Of or belonging to the imaginary island of Utopia or its people.   †**b.** Nowhere existing –1689.   **2.** Impracticably ideal ; of impossible and visionary perfection, esp. in respect of politics, social organization, etc. 1613.   **3.** Indulging in impracticably ideal projects for social welfare, etc. ; believing in or aiming at the perfecting of polity or social conditions 1597.

1. b. In certain intermundane spaces and U. regions without the world 1678.   **2.** When he was laying out so magnificent, charitable, and philosophic an U. villa H. WALPOLE.   An U. sketch of a perfect government 1798.   **3.** You are..a Theoretical Common-wealths-man, an U. Dreamer COWLEY.

B. *sb.* **1.** A native or inhabitant of Utopia ; a dweller in some Utopia 1551.   **2.** One who conceives or proposes schemes for the perfecting of social and political conditions ; an advocate of visionary reform 1873.

2. Utopians who are equally ignorant of capital, labour, or hard work 1887.   Hence **Uto·pianism**, **Uto·pianize** *v. trans.* to render U.   **U·topism** = UTOPIANISM.   **U·topist** = sense B.

I. THE NEW UTOPIANS

Throughout history idealistic and humanistic men have responded to social problems with dreams of imaginary societies where the problems are neatly and abstractly dissolved. The dreams, considered to be impossible by the dreamers themselves, are called "utopias." Men have dreamed utopian dreams most frequently in periods where the subjective and objective factors of the social situation prevented real social change.[1]

Thomas More (1478-1535), reacting to the suffering caused by the beginnings of mercantilism, created *Utopia,* an imaginary, propertyless, classless society where villages scattered throughout the countryside ensured the equal distribution of goods and opportunities among the individual inhabitants.

During the same period on the Continent artists and planners were translating the hierarchical power of state and church into architectural forms. The environments they created both represented their social world and served as powerful instruments for its reproduction.[2] These city environments, as is always the case, represented most intensively the social problems and contradictions which the society had solved and left unsolved.

In France, during the time of enlightenment and the French revolution, utopians projected rational, mathematical, scientific and geometric visions of environments to substitute for the loss of social cohesion and individual salvation.

In the beginning of the 19th century the early *utopian socialists,*[3] concerned with social reforms, the collectivization of property and social life, the reduction of working time and the satisfaction of basic material needs, attempted to incorporate these reforms into rational and geometric plans and projects. Unfortunately, the isolated projects of this "utopian movement" were quickly distorted, absorbed and integrated into the established capitalistic systems. The subsequent attempts to form *garden cities* in the end of the 19th century had a similar destiny. Remaining only small-scale half-realizations, their importance is largely documentary.

The *utopians of the 1920's,* inspired by the Russian revolution, accented the solidarity of the struggling proletariat. They demanded the independence from and abolishment of private capital and the equality and freedom of all people and all labor, liberation from exploitation and a way of life liberated from material miseries where the *realm of necessity and realm of freedom*[4] would be united. These utopians show a great deal of conceptual and social fantasy in their approach to the full integration of human beings and their needs. However, architectural functionalism, developing simultaneously and easily incorporated into the rationalized industrial forces of capitalism repressed the ideas of the utopians. While initially opposing the bourgeois ideology of ornament of the 19th century, functionalism helped to generate the 20th century ideology of *technical rationality* and *functional aestheticism* (form follows function).[5]

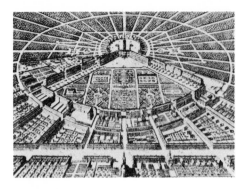

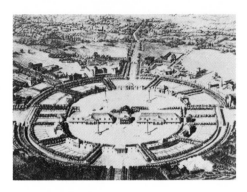

Karlsruhe — Instrument of social reproduction through social control, visual control and symbolism

Ledoux: Ville de Chaux — Visions of geometric environments as substitutes for lost social cohesion

Robert Owen — Cooperative village at the end of the eighteenth century

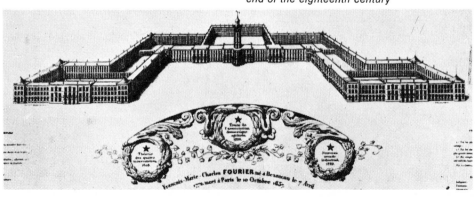

Fourier — Social reforms within a rational geometric framework

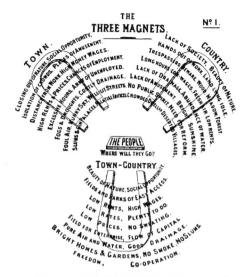

Ebenezer Howard — Theory of the Three Magnets

Letchworth — Small-scale isolated half-realizations

Le Corbusier — Purposive rationality and functional aestheticism easily exploited by capitalism

Kenzo Tange — Model of residential units to be located on Tokyo Bay

Following the second world war a new kind of utopian thinking appeared within capitalist societies resulting in the *real* or *concrete utopias*.[6] These are no longer dreams impossible of fulfillment, but descriptions of not-yet-implemented "realities," proposing to improve our present society, to predict and consciously control the near future. These utopias and their creators, the *"new utopians,"*[7] use the available technological and organizational means and resources to deal with the present problems of our industrial society: the fast development of technology, the slow adaptation of the society, the population and urban explosions, automation, electronization, mass-production, consumption, mobility and so on. Making scientific extrapolations from social trends, the new utopians believe in the possibility of good and immediate solutions. However, they accept the present social structure as "given" and renounce the idea of constructing new social orders.

From this position, new utopian *architects* deluge the world with a flood of quickly-designed environmental proposals: huge monostructural city systems based on the ideologies of physical flexibility, mobility and exchangeability

Archigram — Walking city

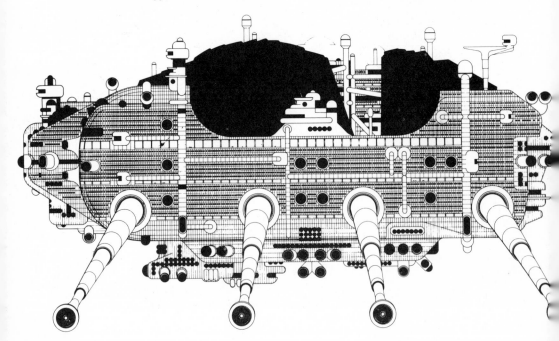

of parts and elements for the sake of mass-production and rationalization; a continuous metamorphosis of traditional technologies and steering systems to form an absolutely variable environment providing for expansion, contraction, movements and adaptations according to simplified and ideologized human needs within a society which is liberated through physical mobility; and the metabolists' mega-structures built over existing cities, lakes, countries and oceans, but preserving traditional and conventional social structures.

"New utopian" *city planners* and social engineers project self-regulating large-scale and complex organic eco-systems and biotectures. They study how to govern continuous complex social and physical environments. They experiment with systems theory and translate the latest results to our present cities, intending to support new directions in city planning: the change from the sequential implementation of unique ideas to a constant *steering* of *tendencies* and *processes;* the change from the practice of pure art and organization to a scientific method of *steering urban systems.* Their basic idea is to liberate society from material and physical restrictions through the implementation of an open, flexible, continually changing and transparent, balanced,

Tool of the social engineers

non-exploited environment which is supposed to stimulate society to change and in turn be changed through society.

New Utopianism, however, since it incorporates the present structure of established social values and contradictions, is inherently unsuited to implement new liberating objectives. It is more likely to produce an outcome similar to that of functionalism, which served the advancement of capitalism rather than humanism. Thus, new utopianism, integrated into capitalism, on the one hand calls for the liberation from material restriction and over-exploitation, on the other hand it ignores the consequence of its projects. Immense consumption, waste and a balanced exploitation of flexible material and energy, essential to an oppressive consumer society, supports a situation where the "haves" exploit the labor of the "have nots" and where individual and collective needs are channeled into class- and mass-oriented "conspicuous consumption" which oppresses people's emotional and mental freedom more than ever. The flexible environment of the future therefore, built upon the present capitalist system, will have enough elbow room for wasteful consumption and exploitation, whereby the new utopians' ideas of human liberation remain an ideology for the textbooks.

The traditional utopias, open to social changes but closed to formal environmental changes, are now replaced by the "new utopias," open to formal environmental changes but closed to social ones. This goes along with the change in the political reality: there are no more tyrants and kings expressing in their oppressive architecture their *centralized hierarchical* ruling power and dominating, with it, the environment. But instead there are power elites expressing in a *functionally oppressive architecture* their *functional ruling power* and dominating, with it, the environment — an environment which in most cases serves the establishment of profitable urban functions and nothing more.

Accordingly, "new utopian" urban planners cannot be understood to be, as they claim, simply organizers and planners of urban functions (the production, distribution and consumption of goods, energy, information and people) or simply as planners of a better environment. In this they labor under a new *utopian illusion,* that their plans are somehow effective and autonomous in themselves.

In fact, however, our "utopian" urban planners are subordinate, financially and ideologically, to the ruling capitalistic elite. In this situation their labor and plans can never be more than instruments for the extension and reproduction of the profit-oriented class system.

Marcuse sees this as unavoidable: "If capitalism does not succeed in exploiting these new possibilities of the productive forces and their organization, the productivity of labor will fall beneath the level required by the rate of profit."[8]

II. PLANNING IN CAPITALISM

I Believe

•

I believe in the supreme worth of the individual and in his right to life, liberty, and the pursuit of happiness.

I believe that every right implies a responsibility, every opportunity, an obligation; every possession, a duty.

I believe that the law was made for man and not man for the law; that government is the servant of the people and not their master.

I believe in the dignity of labor, whether with head or hand; that the world owes no man a living but that it owes every man an opportunity to make a living.

I believe that thrift is essential to well ordered living and that economy is a prime requisite of a sound financial structure, whether in government, business or personal affairs.

I believe that truth and justice are fundamental to an enduring social order.

I believe in the sacredness of a promise, that a man's word should be as good as his bond; that character—not wealth or power or position—is of supreme worth.

I believe that the rendering of useful service is the common duty of mankind and that only in the purifying fire of sacrifice is the dross of selfishness consumed and the greatness of the human soul set free.

I believe in an all-wise and all-loving God, named by whatever name, and that the individual's highest fulfillment, greatest happiness, and widest usefulness are to be found in living in harmony with His will.

I believe that love is the greatest thing in the world; that it alone can overcome hate; that right can and will triumph over might.

—JOHN D. ROCKEFELLER, JR.

NG BODIES was   Jeff Radford, wh
rmer serviceman,   in the Mekong d

Very few "new utopians" give any attention to the consequences of their work on society as a whole. They attempt to confine all criticism to limited discussions of technique. This, of course, is insufficient. We must examine as well the assumptions and motivations underlying their creations. An evaluation that is purely methodological and technocratic accepts a division of natural science from critical social science and fosters the accumulation of irrelevant detailed knowledge. Methodological evaluation by itself creates a false peace and engenders the positivistic circle: innovation — technocratic critique — improvement of the innovation, implying that the innovations are good and acceptable *per se.*

But the goals for which scientific methods are developed, along with the choice of objects under research and the ways in which they are applied, are more influential in determining the effects of a method on society than the method itself. To evaluate and understand systems theory and model building processes as new tools in planning and to evaluate their application to the physical and social system "city," we must first take a long look at the social and political framework[1] within which the planning concepts are to be applied.

Planning and Laissez-Faire Capitalism
The social order of classical capitalism ("liberalism old-style")[2] is the product of a peculiar contradiction. By taking advantage of the dependency of labor on capital the capitalists strive on the one hand for *stability, security, continuity* and a planned undisturbed order of events. On the other hand this system demands *dynamic anarchistic adaptation,* risk-taking, openness and competitive behavior, rewarding with the "transcendental" capitalist's values of accumulated capital, property, power and maximum profits.

To avoid continual conflicts, the philosophical concepts of *"libertarianism"* and of absolute and individual "democratic freedom" are used to cloud the inherent contradictions. These generate certain *normative social patterns:* at the *private level,* the right to absolute individualism, self-aggrandizement, self-determination, self-reliance and individual initiatives; at the *social level,* the right to articulate and follow one's own interests and self-determined group interests and affiliations (the spirit of the community); at the *economic level,* the right of individual profit-maximization, and the "free enterprise and market system" based on individual performance and class origin; and at the *political level,* in the United States, the system of "checks and balances" and the division between the state and federal governments.

Government *competition* with private enterprise and *institutionalized planning* are considered the most dangerous interventions in individual freedom and strong violations of the normative patterns, as the society is assumed to be

---

The Ten Libertarian Commandments of
John D. Rockefeller

11

maintained and developed by the *"hidden hand,"* an automatic reconciliation of *stability* and *dynamic adaptation*. (A strict rejection of planning understood as the first step of intervention is therefore still a conventional value within the present American conservative middle classes.)

Planning on a limited scale is known to be needed, however, and can help to conceal the contradictions between stability and adaptive dynamics. It therefore is tolerated in the following decentralized forms as nonintervention:

Private planning actions to maintain one's own social and economic security: the accumulation of properties and capital.

Public planning action within a democratic process of decision-making: environmental, administrative and security concerns.

Free investment planning action to increase profits and control labor power.

But, in general, we can say that any kind of planning action is restricted and only pertains to isolated parts and elements *without rational relation to the whole society.* The rational character of planning itself thus remains, in the full context, irrational.

The role of the state at this economic stage is restricted to mediating and arbitrating open conflicts and violence that arise between individuals or owners of private capital. Hidden conflicts between classes and dependent labor are assumed to be nonexistent. The state is supposed to react, not to act. Its guarantee of "democratic freedom" functions, however, more ideologically than effectively and draws attention away from inherent class conflicts. In this situation the benefit is on the side of the capitalists as they can force the state, by their power of capital against the dependent labor, to provide for private and profit-oriented rights within the framework of "democratic freedom" and "free enterprise."

From Laissez-Faire Capitalism to Monopoly Capitalism

The first form of serious *state intervention* with the advancing capitalism of the nineteenth century came with the first organized battles of the labor unions against the capitalists in Europe and America. Pressured by organized masses, the state functioned as mediator in daily conflicts working out certain compromises. As a non-organized group, libertarian (or now conservative) American capitalists responded with a wave of anti-interventionism (anti-dirigism).[3] But the technological innovations, the increase in production, the concentration and centralization of capital and the strong organization of the working classes generates a permanent fear among the capitalists of a "general crisis" and of the end of capitalism. In the absence of any automatic guarantee of *order, stability* and its maintenance becomes the major concern of the state apparatus and capitalists, resulting finally in the United States in a collaboration — *organized monopoly capitalism.* Factories and whole industries consolidate into large corporations, trusts and monopolies in order to reduce personal risks, price competition, and other insecurities while maintaining economic continuity and high rates of profit. The control of the individual "owner" is handed over to a "managerial board" which functions anonymously as a representative of capital and constitutes a new managerial elite. This type of organization of capitalism becomes possible only when fewer participants in the market place are responsible for the vital decisions of the capitalist economy; the more monopolization advances, the easier it becomes to build an explicit policy consensus among the major corporate groups. They begin to conceive of their enlightened long-term self-interest in political and administrative rather than in purely economic and market-oriented terms.

Long- and short-range planning, which is essential for effective intervention, becomes the most important element for governing the complex political and economic processes with their continual changes and expansions, and for maintaining the power of the state and the profits of private capital. In taking over the responsibility and permanent control of certain key industries by giving them tax shelter, continuous armament contracts and investment incentives, the state takes action to intervene and indirectly controls the desperately needed stabilization and maintenance of the economic cycle.[4]

The goals of planned state-capital interventions filtered through the state's institutions are both functional and ideological. The functional goals are: to provide for regulated, organized market conditions; to implement long- and short-range programs for the absorption of surplus capital while maintaining the existing class structure and the finance aristocracy; to provide conditions for stable economic growth; to encourage the development of system-adapted planning partners; and to take action against every appearing crisis or recession with all available means — including armed intervention in foreign countries.

The *ideological* goals of state-capital planning are: to provide a psychological rationalization for the new economic order; to avoid any kind of open conflicts; to provide for the maintenance of the bourgeois-democratic value system and the existing class structure.

But the introduction of the new economic order does not lead to a new social order. The economic programs set in motion by capital and state are legitimized with ideological "secondary arguments" taken from the treasure box of the democratic value system.[5] Pride in the new technical achievements and programs skillfully directs attention away from the change in the economic order. After the depression, the Federal highway and public works programs created some jobs and new industries but mostly served to stabilize the economy and insure the continuity of profits while destroying the environment.

The effect of state-capital intervention in the *micro-economic sect*or shows up in industrial rationalization and automation. These seem to increase the continuity and rate of profits and production power.

The development of systematized and automated production machinery generates horizontal production processes involving less human labor power as time progresses. Working people in the machinery of semi-automation become slaves, and in full automation they are a substitute for complex and expensive control mechanisms. Their individual responsibilities and opportunities for failure however increase. Therefore quota controls, required adaptation of people to machines and their rules, specified patterns of behavior and incentives for advancement have become the means to reduce the risks for the capital owner. Face to face controls are replaced by *structural* and *normative imperatives*. Science in its dependence on capital becomes the most important factor in production, as the basis for technological advancement, technical rationalization and human control, and as the source of production growth and the anticipation of conflicts between people and machines.

Planning, at least short-range planning, is usually given to a group of experts and decision-makers (in the micro-economic field most often to specialists commissioned to analyze, specialize and rationalize the decision and production process). *Participation* by non-experts, of course, is excluded *per se.* Data and information processing, storage, distribution and concentration, and the fast-channeled and frictionless flow of information between machines and

workers are the primary conditions necessary for the maintenance and growth of production processes. The human being as the mediator of information is eliminated. Information becomes invisible.

Rationalization[6] becomes a principle of optimized systematic and technical production and reproduction which no longer applies only to production and administration processes. Developing its own dynamism, rationalization extends to the whole society and subordinates every individual at every level to its principles. The framework of the capitalist society becomes a rationalized industrial and state system under and in which the individual, forced to adapt, becomes caught, exploited and objectified. While self-determination and individual freedom for the labor-dependents became more and more limited by the *imperative of rationalization* brought about by this distorted and reduced rationality and by the *state and capital controlled intervention*, again the conservative ideologies of libertarianism gain new functional importance: they should make their prisoners believe that with no chance for its realization, they still possess the right for freedom and self-determination.

Planning in Late Capitalism
Since early in the century, the task of American leaders has been to make "peace," "self-determination" and the promise of a better life the language that explains American purposes. Probably none of them has ever willfully deprived a man of food or killed another in cold blood; they order political and economic suppression and murder — by gas, napalm, or nuclear weapons — only as a means of realizing peace and preserving democracy.[7]

The phase of U.S. capitalism after World War II is characterized by a *liberalism new style*[8] — fragmented attempts to bring about economic redistribution, a participatory democracy and a liberal welfare and warfare capitalism. After labor unions were legitimized during the 1930's, reforms were instituted to attain social and economic "justice." Welfare legislation, social security laws, the Civil Rights Bill and the anti-poverty war and community action programs appeared.

But as most *ad hoc* legislation brings no immediate and visible profits the programs end in illusion and tokenism: now the unions are an integrated part of the system, and the problems of increasing unemployment, housing and transportation shortages, inadequate health and education services and increasing racial tensions are still unsolved. Over *thirty million* Americans, including over *forty per cent* of the Black population, now live under the poverty level. *Twenty per cent* of all families receive only *five per cent* of the total income while the top *twenty per cent* receive over *forty per cent*. Profits still accrue only to a small minority of the population: *eighty per cent* of all corporate stock is owned by only *one per cent* of the American people.[9] Seen in this context the "great society" and the "welfare state" are illusions. As the society grows richer the pressure on the "have-nots" continues and even increases.

What remains is welfare misuse[10] as does welfare-bureaucratism, -professionalism, control over and subjection of the poor, while the real subsidies go to the middle class capitalists, professionals, house-builders, businessmen and bankers.

It is the belief in our commitment to welfare that, more than anything else, allows our honorable men to sleep at night while other men are murdered, jailed or hungry.[11]

15

"Ineffective" and urgent demands of the oppressed people

The tremendous increase in productive power, achieved through the full integration of technology and science now introduces a new dimension of marketing, based on manipulated *"effective demands"* and financial abilities, ignoring authentic *urgency.* Scientific marketing research, studies in behavioral sciences, decision theory, psychology and medicine are utilized in a huge need-stimulation industry that in turn provides a secure, stabilized and class-oriented consumption. The actual *"user needs"* and needs of those people who cannot demand effectively enough are consciously eliminated.[12]

It is a society in which the ruling class does not so much cause material misery for the oppressed but instead brings about a growing alienation; it is an environment in which the ego and the superego is increasingly manipulated in the interests of the ruling classes in such a way that the ego is on one hand weakly developed and that on the other hand new needs are constantly being generated without concern for the existing still unsatisfied ones. It leads to a complex of needs which contradict each other so that the satisfaction of an essential part of needs cannot be progressively met but rather regressively, that means through repression.[13]

The cycle of production — consumption — surplus distribution now is completely controlled by a new alliance, capital — state — science. The *surplus distribution* (based on an ideologized belief in technological advancement) is directed toward prestigious capital-intensive programs: road construction, space and war adventures, armies and bureaucracies. The state becomes the largest consumer and employer. It

The "effective" demands of the middle-classes

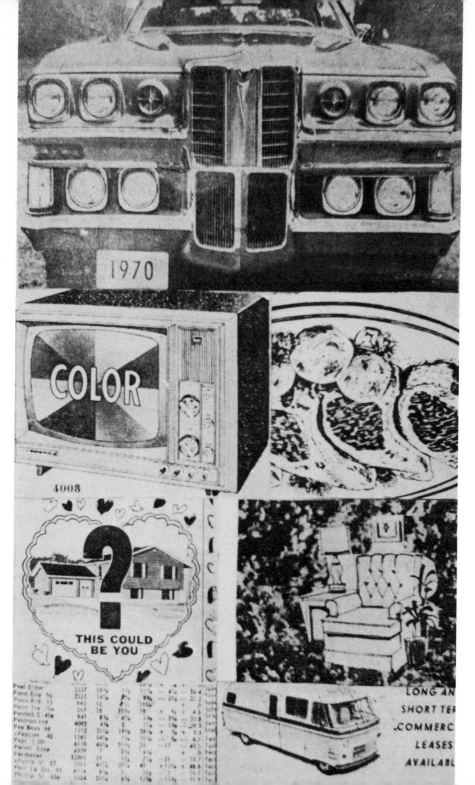

etroit Insists the Future Will Be Cars, Cars, Ca

For I looked into the future
Far as human eye could see,
Saw a vision of the world
And all the wonder that would be.

Saw the freeway filled with traffic,
No mass transit, only cars,
200 million Fords and Chevys,
The urban planners drunk in bars.

—*Detroit Doggerel*

Road, car, oil and gas consumption — A prestigious capital-intensive program

covers specific unpredictable lags in demands.[14] Its war industry alone entangles increasingly other industries and almost all universities.[15]

Derived from war research and economics, new stability-oriented planning and intervention methods become the most important element at all social and technical levels. Information theory, decision theory, power theory, systems theory, cybernetics, operational research, computer programming etc., are the names and rational elements of new purposive-oriented[16] planning techniques.

Despite these advances in planning techniques, planning processes are still irrational. Hundreds of irrational and uncontrolled influences become absorbed by filtering out alternatives with technically rational or socially irrational criteria, by accepting the imperatives of state and corporate capital interests or by subconscious and conscious manipulation from personal and group interests.

Similarly, the new overactive planning stance of the government is subject to these irrational influences. However, the complex dependencies entangling capital, state, sciences and bureaucracies call for control and a new framework of economic order. Military, education and transportation problems become so huge and complex that they can only be dealt with under government direction. Planning as a method of anticipated control and regulation seems to be the only sensible means of maintaining economic and social order.

In addition, planning imperatives are recognized as powerful instruments for manipulation and as offensive weapons against crises of any kind. They camouflage skillful conflict-avoiding mechanisms. They can be used for justification and objectification of political moves and as the means for indirect invisible power mediation.

With these developments a change in the middle and upper classes occurs. They give up their general hostility to planning without discussion, shifting closer to the bourgeois principle of status security. The loss of a realistic "democratic freedom" and individualism seems not so painful. Even when affected in their own individual spheres, they simply ignore the fact of permanent state interventions. For the state, this change means that there is no more need to show a specific regard for laissez-faire liberals.

Now the government simultaneously initiates and justifies its centralized planning. However, the principles of efficiency and the strategy of purposive-functional program planning are restricted to specific sectors and programs:

In the economic sphere *purposive economic programs* such as tax policies, the determination of surplus absorption, subsidies for specific industries, the funding of private corporations for research and development.

In the social sphere, *conditioning programs* including emergency legislation, the maintaining of police armies, class-oriented court activities, repressive school systems and welfare programs which secure the maintenance of the socio-economic order and prevent open conflicts.

In the case of threats from inside or outside, the state is prepared to apply drastic measures; to restrict basic freedoms and human rights and implement exact and permanent control actions based on *prefabricated preprogrammed plans.* These strategic actions eliminate unknown and fluctuating variables, for the effectiveness of total centralized intervention is based on the skillful manipulation of known variables.

Integrated war industry — The base of the U.S. economy

The Trillion-Dollar Investme

federal budget $148 billion

DO YOU KNOW HE COSTS OF WAR?

FISCAL YEAR 1969

The U.S. has poured more than one trillion dollars into the ni since the end of World War II. One-tenth of this staggering a was invested in the Vietnam war.

70% to the military to pay for wars past and present

Out of every tax dollar in Fiscal Year 1969, 70¢ went to p wars, past and present, and preparation for war.

Of this amount, 19¢ went to pay for Vietnam, 35¢ for other c military expenditures, and 16¢ for the cost of past wars.

Every man, woman and child in the U.S. is now spending an age of $400 a year on the military, an increase of 60% ov last five years.

Only 14.5% to health, education and welfare

other 15.5%

On the other hand, rational planning and interventions for *human needs* remain mysterious monsters. Unknown variables remain unknown. The state-capital coalition has no motivation to know more about the destiny of people as long as they keep quiet. Only pressure in a crisis situation sets the state bureaucracy in motion. When pressure is reduced, the state's care for people disappears. Permanent pressure on the state, however, comes from the capitalists who have the power to use the institutions of the state for their own interests.

The capitalists determine the use of planning and investments in those sectors where good and permanent profit is expected and where the economists, technocrats, bureaucrats and war planners can avoid participation and controls by concerned people.

The *nonprofessionals* and *people concerned* in the implemented interventions and plans, however, experience most planning as both given and rational. On the other hand, confronted with the final products and solutions, they feel alienated and trapped within the established structural imperatives. Nonalienation and understanding would require *general and active participation* in the production and planning process. General participation, however, is contradictory to the whole capitalistic structure where economic planning decisions are made by the elite and by corporations using their greatest power of intervention, the power of investment decision. This power, according to Andrew Hacker,

> *. . . will determine the quality of life for a substantial segment of society. Men and materials will move across continents; old communities will decay and new ones will prosper; tastes and habits will alter; new skills will be demanded, and*

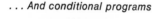

. . . And conditional programs

the education of a nation will adjust itself accordingly; even government will fall into line, providing public services that corporate developments make necessary.[17]

Within the *totality* of the new capitalistic "System," individual freedom and the implementation of democratic rights as effective citizen feedback disappear.[18] There is almost no escape from structural and normative imperatives, physical, psychological and economic dependencies. Human beings must adapt themselves to the given framework.

The philosopher and psychoanalyst R. D. Laing[19] states that in order to maintain the atrocities of the modern capitalistic world, it is necessary for men to destroy their capacity to see clearly what is around them and hide from the horrors which they commit and are forced to commit. The ease with which people can delude themselves about the true character of the world comes from the split between the *"inner"* and an *"outer"* self.

The inner self of a "normal" person is usually greatly concealed — even from himself — and is seen only by imagination, fantasy and dreams. The outer self, which Laing calls the "false self system," is the person's active personality. People's actions in the outer world are for the most part mechanical and so they do not feel a need to attack or destroy an alien reality within themselves. The person's well-exercised social personality engulfs his total system and so he loses his critical potentiality. True possibilities for him to spontaneously manifest in action a personal definition of whom or what he wishes to be cease to exist.

For the middle classes, a few status functions such as car and job mobility, the possession of property or land and

---

Products of social conditioning programs

the ideology of free choice replace the consciousness of misery. The loss of individual responsibility, the loss of privacy and identity and the loss of human capability for active communication, all brought about by the powerful institutions of state and capital and controlled by skillful scientific means, constitute organized, militant, permanent violence against people and eliminate even a desire for freedom and citizen feedback which goes beyond the freedom from material scarcity and austerity.

This human tragedy is the result of a system which is purposely organized to exploit and sometimes to create the weaknesses of its individuals. It is a system in which planning and intervention in favor of a more human life for its citizens can play no central role, since this would threaten its essentially exploitative structure. Consequently, certain basic and social needs must be ignored; or, if they are brought to public attention, their discussion is used as an ideological tool to continually renew the peoples' hopes without implementing real social change. Thus politicians endlessly promise sufficient jobs, decent health services for all, useful leisure activities, and effective planning of cities, housing and mass transportation; promises which have not been and cannot be fulfilled within the American capitalistic system. The sporadic, isolated and anarchistic welfare experiments are anything but workable solutions to handle these problems and meet the human needs which stand behind and beyond them.

III. IMPERATIVES IN URBAN PLANNING

Environmental and Structural Imperatives

The built world is organized to support the growth of society, as the natural world is organized to supply agricultural produce. And extending our "false analogy," as the farmer works with nature, so must the citizen learn to control the beneficent and malignant forces in the urban context so that, through urban husbandry, they may create a place and a climate in which their society will thrive.

But the urban physical environment — the framework for urban life — basically does not grow, change or thrive by itself. Iron and stones do not move themselves. The urban environment needs social and physical planning, i.e. the organization of urban complex systems. *And* it needs energy which is provided by *people's work* and machines; or more generally, by the social order which determines the priorities for the use of energy. The physical environment and the social order interact with each other similarly in a feedback structure, but with built-in resistances which set limits on environmental control. The resistances result from the social order and not from the existing environment, since our present available technical materials and intellectual means[2] allow almost any conceivable change within the technical and natural environments.

We call these resistances *structural imperatives:* forces arising from previously established social structures which seem to limit the directions and possibilities for environmental change or non-change, conceptual reorientation and redetermination. They are historically determined but also historically mutable (e.g. zoning laws).

American urban planners are faced with five main groups of imperatives limiting their action: historical, irrational, normative, political, and institutional.

Historical Imperatives

The founding fathers, when they conceived the new republic, considered cities as places which undermined moral health and freedom. Understanding their new society as basically agrarian, they gave most attention and political power to the rural constituents. In this way they believed they could moderate the growth of cities.

The continuing imbalance of political power and representation between the urban vs. suburban and rural constituencies leaves the cities in a powerless situation and with a dependency on federal and state governments.[3]

For these political reasons the government takes no action to restrict the ever-increasing ghettoization of affluent suburban and of poor inner city communities and there are neither plans nor means to make cities viable as whole environments. While needed transitions from a once rural to an urban society are still being ignored billions for highways are arbitrarily allocated.[4]

Irrational Imperatives

The capitalistic "state planning," through its part-interventionism, incorporates irrationality into all its planning processes with a view to maintaining its present system-stability. We find the same attitudes toward planning at the local level, but for different reasons. There it stems from the ideology of "individualism" in the American conservative middle classes who are still the most influential force on planning in communities, and the fear of a misused and misleading centralism. As a result there is a general hostility to planning which allows only *advisory planning,* supporting the random cooperation between the people who commission plans and those who execute them.

The planner himself selling his labor to capital is caught between contradictory interests. There are the planner's individual interests: as a member of an economic class and of a professional peer group, as a competing member of the current planning and architectural ideologies, as an artist intervening in and organizing the environment. He is also subject to the conflicting interests of his clients. He must collaborate either with his *sponsor clients* (the public and private institutions) or the *user clients* (the people concerned).[5]

Planning itself has *no* institutional anchorage,[6] *no* protection in law and *no* power *per se.* It is understood as being part of the economic environmental production process; its subordination under production and economic imperatives is basically accepted. Pressures of time, profit interests, scarcity of means and the dependence on funding prevent the adoption of long-range or comprehensive planning methods. Essential research on basic human needs or "multi-dimensional" planning preparation is obviously not possible. *Public institutions* which could provide such information do not exist; independent research becomes too expensive. Only huge *private* organizations can afford research. They make their profit by selling information second-hand.

The partial solution, the *ad hoc* solution, the "one-dimensional" solution, short-range solutions and emergency repairs are the outcome, implemented by an army of "one-dimensional" experts who organize, without feeling any doubts, the merely routine, rationalized, optimized solutions.

Normative Imperatives

Although there are no laws regulating planning procedures themselves, we find three different standards, or norms, being used in formulating planning processes.

1. The *detail-oriented,* one-dimensional *technocratic standard*[7] is adequate for technological rationalized problem-solving, mostly used for architectural problems. The production of the planning document is the most important stage, since the set of planning goals is to find the "objective," economically optimized solution. Accuracy, technical precision, determination of all steps and parts and detailed instructions are the values for measuring its success. Every irregularity and deviation is excluded by precise model thinking. Implementation, once decided, must be executed. Changes become impossible. The technocratic concept follows the philosophy of *"muddling through"*[8] (incrementalism).

2. The *flexible structural standard* allows for continual changes during the whole planning process and after its implementation. The plan is less product and more historical by-product. Continuity of implementation is the planning program. Environmental changes, whether planned or accidental, are supposed to be easily integrated into the planning process. In practice, however, other imperatives restrict the planned flexibility, with the result that these plans and their products in actual functioning are technocratic, too.

3. A third standard is known but impossible to implement in the present Amer-

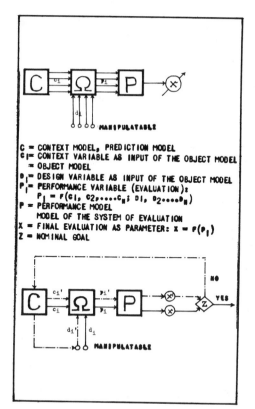

C = CONTEXT MODEL, PREDICTION MODEL
c_i = CONTEXT VARIABLE AS INPUT OF THE OBJECT MODEL
Ω = OBJECT MODEL
D_i = DESIGN VARIABLE AS INPUT OF THE OBJECT MODEL
P_i = PERFORMANCE VARIABLE (EVALUATION):
$P_i = P(c_1, c_2, \ldots c_n; D_1, D_2, \ldots D_n)$
P = PERFORMANCE MODEL
MODEL OF THE SYSTEM OF EVALUATION
X = FINAL EVALUATION AS PARAMETER: $X = P(P_i)$
Z = NOMINAL GOAL

Model of the "conflict generation machine"
(Rittel)

ican society. The *comprehensive plan,* a plan considering all available technical and societal data — sociological, political, psychological, etc. — is based on the idea of rational and need-oriented societal planning.

The planning-for-the-whole[9] approach, is impossible because the planner is neither able nor willing to evaluate the complex plan nor to set priorities, other than economic data, against it. An emergency call for aid from sociologists has ended with disappointment and new problems. Empirical critical sociology, capable only of exposing present problems, cannot deliver the required normative evaluation method. Plans pre-

tending to be comprehensive, therefore, usually are nothing other than flexible technocratic-economic plans determined by business interests which, in turn, follow the leadership of their pragmatic economists.[10]

Political Imperatives

The lack of legitimate centralized planning leaves most planning decisions formally and politically at local levels. Accordingly, within the realm of his technical advice, the planner is forced to decide also political questions; without, however, the help of supportive public institutions. The *liberal planner* sometimes feels that he is strong enough to do this job. But the *conservative middle-class planner* is very insecure about the task. First, because he would like to practice "value-free," "rational" and "rationalized" planning — as long as it is well removed from politics and personal responsibility. Second, because he traditionally suspects representative democracy from which he actually legitimizes his position and his power. And thirdly, because he feels unhappy about the existence of a critical concerned public that could provide him with general criteria for the evaluation of planning goals and planning results. Nevertheless he internalizes this situation as a given fact of life.

These insecurities make planners completely dependent on their planning commissioners and on their social and ideological value systems. Elbow room for explicit personal political decisions is excluded. This situation has positive effects on the people concerned within the affluent communities, as these people are virtually identical with the commissioner of the plans. Within the poor communities, however, the people concerned become objects of alienation, oppression and exploitation, as they are neither the owners of property and land nor commissioners or executers of the plans. The liberal planners who suffer

27

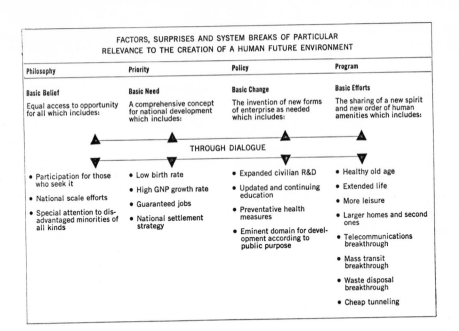

FACTORS, SURPRISES AND SYSTEM BREAKS OF PARTICULAR
RELEVANCE TO THE CREATION OF A HUMAN FUTURE ENVIRONMENT

Philosophy	Priority	Policy	Program
Basic Belief	**Basic Need**	**Basic Change**	**Basic Efforts**
Equal access to opportunity for all which includes:	A comprehensive concept for national development which includes:	The invention of new forms of enterprise as needed which includes:	The sharing of a new spirit and new order of human amenities which includes:

THROUGH DIALOGUE

- Participation for those who seek it
- National scale efforts
- Special attention to disadvantaged minorities of all kinds

- Low birth rate
- High GNP growth rate
- Guaranteed jobs
- National settlement strategy

- Expanded civilian R&D
- Updated and continuing education
- Preventative health measures
- Eminent domain for development according to public purpose

- Healthy old age
- Extended life
- More leisure
- Larger homes and second ones
- Telecommunications breakthrough
- Mass transit breakthrough
- Waste disposal breakthrough
- Cheap tunneling

Characteristic of pragmatism — Pretended agreements through lack of strategies

from these confining dependencies feel relief at the introduction of occasional citizen participation and community action programs (CAP) for the poor communities, welcomed as the "breakthrough" to integrate politically the users of the plan. Unfortunately, *citizen participation* in this case, is not what it appears or what it should be, i.e., effective non-alienated participation of citizens concerned in decision-making processes that affect their lives. Instead the concept is used for publicly legitimizing all kinds of interventions, for collecting information used for social control and for the reaffirming political planning contents and planning steps. With this ploy, the planner and professionals formally yield their political responsibility. They believe themselves to be free again and retire to the "neutralized professional background,"[11] from which they can overwhelm the people concerned with their expertise. Fortunately, such experiences have made people wary so that they tend to keep away from this kind of participation, thus practicing a kind of passive resistance, evidence of the failure of the Community Action Program[12] and the Model City.[13]

These disorganized, centralized programs, however, make all localized planning action insecure. Random and arbitrary shortages and cutbacks of federal funds prevent long-range planning. They also reach the middle classes first for management[14] and distribution, providing thereby additional resources for control of the lower classes. Consequently the middle classes make considerable extra profits, as is demonstrated by most federally supported housing projects. And finally, when funds do arrive, they must be spent under pressure and in a raging hurry.

Institutional Imperatives
In most European countries there are

decentralized state planning departments which control the development and implementation of plans. In the U.S. such institutions are virtually non-existent. However, the situation itself generates a different kind of imperative. On one side there is a narrow set of established and institutionalized rights and values (e.g. property rights) but on the other side planning is "free" without any institutional protection or restriction. This becomes a source of many social conflicts.

A weak form of institutionalized planning exists in the *Planning Commission,* originally introduced in order to protect the middle classes against the increasing power of new immigrants and against corrupt planning actions. The Planning Commission's power, however, is very limited and only applicable in small communities. In addition, criticism by the liberals of its aristocratic and repressive character has recently prevented it from acting in important decisions.

Other forms of institutionalized planning in the form of City Councils and State Departments of Planning have been developed in a few cases. Most planning action, however, has been taken over by local organizations commissioned by the city governments or private groups and supported by Federal Housing and Urban Development organs. These latter only fund plans according to principles of effective rationalization and profit-maximization.

The Fall into Method Production Versus the Establishment of New Institutions

In general we can say that the American planner is less restricted by normative imperatives than by irrational and political ones. There are basically two strategies to make possible new and liberating planning actions within the present order. The first would establish publicly controlled planning institutions and would institutionalize planning itself.[15] The second would develop rationalized

planning methods which could guarantee the implementation of plans while avoiding greater conflicts. As this second alternative is more in keeping with the general philosophy of old-style American liberalism, most efforts focus on a variety of different planning methods and theories: normative formal theories such as systems analysis, feedback and feedforward, model building and evaluation, planning-programming-budgeting, cost-benefit analysis etc. These are being related to or integrated into computer models and technologies, into empirical surveys, codings, into sociological trend and participation models and even into advocacy planning, "ombudsmen"[16] and citizen feedback.

The basic hope of planners is that the introduction of "objective" and "value-free" methods will bring about the desired elbow room to develop higher quality in plans and will afford protection against unprogrammed influences within the planning processes. Although initially the new methods may bring relief from pressures of time and politics, the relief is of short duration. The methods are finally used to reduce planning time and to keep out politics rather than to improve the quality of planning products themselves. Consequently the planner is subordinated again to the same, but now extended, structural and methodical imperatives. Ruled by the method itself, he is and remains a pure technocrat.

Technocracy and Technocratic Planning

The basis of technocratic planning is the positivistic theory of cognition, which divides scientific activities into theory-building and practice, method and content, cognition and action, science and politics, the realm of necessity and the realm of freedom. Accordingly, there is a strict division between *research-subject* (the commissioner, the researcher, the executor) and *research-object* (the given object, the social or environmental problem, the ones concerned and the user). General observations are formulated as hypotheses which must be proved with accepted normative or empirical methods, experiments or argumentation. Proved hypotheses advance to the status of theories. Finally their correctness is corroborated by as many equal repetitions in practice as possible. Then practice, developing its own self-dynamic with little regard for theory, is carried out by designated "experts." The basic premise and simultaneously the ideal image is the *neutral* and objective research-subject. Terrified that he might express his personal values or social position, the "neutral scientist" hides behind the generally accepted theory constructions, scientific methods and methods of implementation. He allows only strict objectivity, matter-of-factness, logical "scientifically provable" arguments to appear within the spectrum of his experiences, categories and interests.

Again and again he reminds us of the inhuman consequences of such planning ideologies. Therefore he excludes all transcendental thinking from his activities and thought processes. Social or political events, he claims, do not exist — aside from those that have already happened.

He ignores the fact that the common methods of research and implementation already contain built-in social values and that he himself, adapted to them, injects these values into his own professional methodology. The "expert" (the pure physical engineer and planner) is in a worse situation. Not knowing where the methods come from, blindly using and accepting them as "value-free," he understands technological advancement as an autonomous, continuous scientific development. Critiques not concerned with objective facts remain irrelevant to him. The social consequences and by-consequences of technological advances are left uncon-

sidered. Rational social criticism is usually neglected under the label "unqualified argumentation."

Technocrats accept their environment with all its structural imperatives as a given-fact. Society is declared to be a "black-box" whose inputs and outputs can be analyzed according to trial and error. To manipulate the box without understanding its inner mechanisms, the technocrat develops techniques — push-button-politics — dominated and devised by systems thinking. Change is understood to be a purely technological process, a matter of the skillful handling of existing structural imperatives.

New social values and internalizations are substituted for those which must be repressed. Socially conditioned stresses on the individual are transformed into positive social values with labels like "personal performance," "stability" and "technical achievement." With these values in their pockets, the technocrats ride busily through a chaotic and insecure world. Security, continuity, stabilization, conflict-avoidance are the values which they impose and with which they intervene. Social elements, organizations, industries, parties and individuals now subordinated to a "political/bureaucratic" order should, they say, be integrated into the system-stabilizing economic order with its conflict-avoiding mechanisms. People, understood as unreliable and unpredictable elements, must be formed into system-conforming parts.

When the technocrats leave the field of their completed activities, we find, added to the old structural resistances, new imperatives, more powerful and more overwhelming. Strategic and instrumental planning and evaluation methods fit very well into a general technocratic world image.

Rationalized, purposive methods, techniques and technologies build the base for technified domination and silent interventions. They deliver the values, criteria, and legitimation of planning decisions, the so-called "neutral values." Liberal politicians integrate system-conforming technocratic developments into their strategies and make their political decisions seem legitimate by pointing to the existing structural imperatives and scientific methods. These are designed to analyze the current structures as given and, simultaneously, to define the best alternatives for further political-technocratic interventions. Their goal is "government by anticipation, rather than by crisis." [17] Extrapolating this situation, we approach a universal technological imperative, established and institutionalized as a self-regulating value system — the situation is an *absolute technocracy*. Society then becomes and is accepted as a system-stabilizing machine, represented and reproduced by an enormous number of structural imperatives. Organized supply and demand markets, once based on price competition, are replaced by innovative markets which are considered to be the actual agents of society. Social needs have to adapt to randomly arriving innovations. Vital needs for joy, happiness and clear awareness are, as Marcuse says, repressed. Technical instruments become new possibilities for repression by domination. Decisions are made by "value-free" decision machines in "push-button-politics." Democratic control over the means of production becomes irrelevant. Democracy is restricted to numerical applause or silent resentment. The "utopian technocrats," however, believe that these trends are favorable to their humanistic ideals. But they feel opposed by politicians. By working for and extrapolating the present self-dynamic technocratic tendencies, they hope to realize their dreams of interventions: man, liberated by technological means, will eliminate the politicians and their hostility to technocratic visions.

However, contrary to these expectations, recent radical criticism proceeds from the assumption that the present structural imperatives are actually the product of ideologies internalized to maintain technological advances in the interests of the present ruling elites. Structural and even technological imperatives and interventions are actually changeable, removable and replaceable according to basic human needs. The radical social scientist, Claus Offe, points out that the present coalition of technocrats and liberal politicians has no future in any case. Interventions based on pure technocratic, administrative and manipulative planning are no longer practical or powerful enough in the face of the rapidly increasing political and social consciousness of concerned people. A growing proportion of people are already beginning to boycott purely technocratic solutions.

Pragmatic Planning
Pragmatic planning, the tradition in most Western democracies, comes from the assumption that structural imperatives must be accepted at first but can be slowly changed according to generally acknowledged maxims. Pragmatic changes start with a critical analysis of the present state of affairs and develop from those through a positive analysis for a better future state. The pragmatic decision model based on "human insights and agreements" is the only possible way to reconstruct a *"critical public"* as proposed by Jürgen Habermas. He therefore demands a dissolution of the role-division between scientist and politician and the establishment of a permanent voluntary dialogue between them. Generalization and simplification is expected to make needs explicit and understandable. Then new theories and common strategies to meet the needs of the people can be set up.

This model is criticised as useless by Claus Offe:

How can the bureaucracies bristling with knowledge and expertise be forced institutionally to start a dialogue with myriad agencies which are there to articulate social needs — namely the political groups — if the bureaucracy itself tends to make the existence of political groups superfluous? [18]

Formal normative mechanisms which generate an artificial dialogue are presently being invented. Horst Rittel, for example, developing the concept of "activity-science" as neither value-free nor dependent on structural imperatives, has conceived of the decision-process as a scientific object, too. He constructs a formalistic model which determines exactly all important steps and decisions in planning or decision processes. Within this framework a group of people — planners, politicians, scientists and people affected by a project — are forced to begin a discussion, creating a *conflict-generation machine*. Arguments generate conflicts and bring the problems to the level of consciousness. Then the best and most representative argument, determined by statistical and formal methods, decides the issue and wins the battle.

When this model is transferred to planning, it becomes a social scientific game. Certain rules and programs must be mastered to play it well; good for the experts who know them; they will probably win the game. They again have the knowledge to manipulate and decide. They can misuse the unequal psychological position of the non-expert game-members and the disadvantages at which non-professionals and ordinary citizens find themselves. In addition, if game decisions are actually questioning existing structural imperatives, there remains still the old question: how can one insure implementations of possibly "non-profit" or "non-economic" but human-oriented planning decisions?

C. West Churchman, operational researcher and himself a pragmatist, complains in a commentary on the collaboration between architecture and operational research about an inherent contradiction within pragmatism when he says:

I said the operational researcher is honest and so, I suppose, is the architect. But there is a more general consideration, and that is morality, and in particular the moral prescription which tells us not to use people as means only. I think both architecture and operations research fail to follow this moral duty. As professions, both should be moral, and are not. Perhaps this is because we are forced by circumstances (managers and owners) to use people, but this is no excuse. [19]

This contradiction, however, is inherent, because conflicts and problems are solved in favor of those who have the "qualified," "better" and "value-free" arguments; namely, those from the ruling classes who possess power, knowledge and money at once — the economists, the technocrats, the professionals, the politicians, the "haves" and not the "have-nots." Pragmatism is subordinated to the priorities and the goal-and-efficiency criteria of the economists and engineers, the technocrats of the capitalistic order.

The actual helplessness of the pragmatists is ironically summarized when Alex Tzonis says:

The academic impartiality and the fear of value judgements degenerated into the remarkable banality of the fetishism of the facts. Levittowns were good, but slums were good too, together with mobile homes. Above all, Los Angeles was good because people moved there, and highways were good, since cars passed through. Everything was good because it reflected different life styles. [20]

IV. INTRODUCTION TO SYSTEMS THINKING

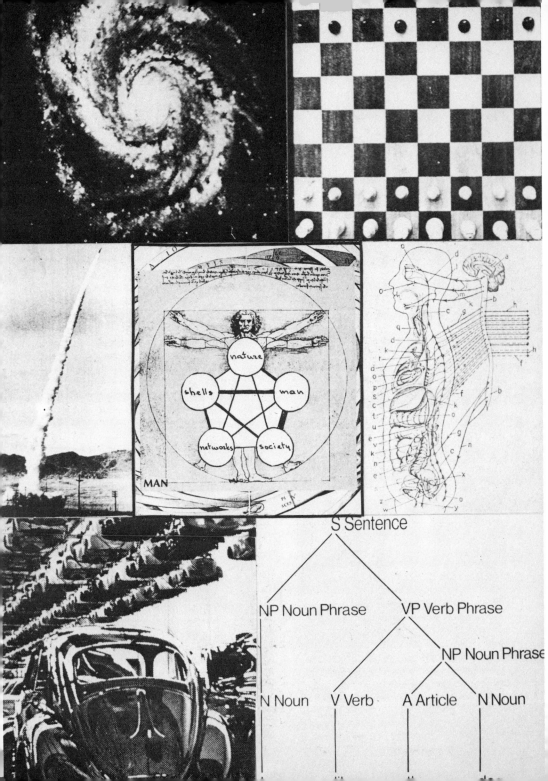

MAN

nature

shells   man

networks   society

S Sentence

NP Noun Phrase   VP Verb Phrase

NP Noun Phrase

N Noun   V Verb   A Article   N Noun

When Albert Einstein defined material as concentrated energy, the nature of interest in theoretical knowledge changed radically. $E = Mc^2$ is more than a formula; it means that matter and energy are no longer opposites, that all facts and processes can be described uniformly in relation to their common basis, that changes are continuous and are caused by an exchange of energy, that the only continuity is change and that the description of facts is always a cut-out from a continuing process; a blow to traditional scientific methods, only used to describe isolated phenomena within our world!

The Natural Scientific disciplines were the first to integrate the understanding of facts and processes with structural principles. Scientists conceive the objects that they study to be *real* or *formal systems.*[1] Insights and laws are represented within a comprehensive framework which is the *abstract model* of the system. The abstract systems are used to measure, to locate, to manipulate resources, energies, facts and components, their functions and relations.

Component or elemental parts of systems can form another system, called a *subsystem.* Subsystems in turn can be divided into subsubsystems, subsubsystems into subsubsubsystems and so on. Since every system is connected to or is part of another system, according to the infinite number of possible *system realizations,* numbers and hierarchies

Man surrounded by an infinite number of systems

of systems are infinite. The biggest unit then is the universe.

The cooperation of the system components is more than simply their addition: there is a *synergistic* effect, an effect only conceivable as a whole. To understand and describe systems *functionally,* it is more essential to disclose the system's *structure,* its *environment,* its *resources,* its *objectives* and its *behavior* than its individual *components.* This requires the tracing of energy and information within the systems, their reception, storage, conversion, delivery and direction, and the understanding of the dialectical relationships between the abstract model and the real system, their simultaneous efficiencies and dependencies. Not the *what* and *why,* but *how* the systems work is the analysts' interest.

Man is always surrounded by an infinite number of systems. There are environmental, natural and artificial systems, technical systems, social systems, organizational systems, projective systems, political systems, control systems, security systems, visual systems, sound systems, electronic systems and so on. They are abstract and real, static and dynamic, simple and complex, open and closed.[2] Liberated from the power of natural systems, man's attention turns fully to artificial systems generated by himself.[3] These, in turn, subordinate him under a new kind of oppression and dependency. But man recognizes only those systems with which he interacts, with or without his volition, consciously or subconsciously. Then, changing the

35

VOLITION
DESIRE
INTENTION
RESOLVE

causes action
or series of
actions

WHICH LEADS
TO A new state
of the world
CONSONANT
WITH VOLITION

a

GOAL ACHIEVING:
THE STANDARD APPROACH
TO HUMAN ACTIVITY

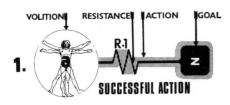

VOLITION   RESISTANCE   ACTION   GOAL

1. R·1

SUCCESSFUL ACTION

2. R·2

UNSUCCESSFUL ACTION

3. SURROGATE GOAL

R·3

DEVIANT ACTION

RESISTANCE OF
THE AMBIENT UNIVERSE
TO PURPOSIVE ACTION

world means to change and control the systems by intervening in the *status quo*. The systems in turn, cause *positive liberating* or *negative restricting and oppressing* interferences in man himself — or both in one (like the transpor-

tation systems). However, systems which were once liberating can turn in time into oppressive systems, and, conversely, oppressive systems into liberating systems — both systems being those imposed on man or generated and used by man. His freedom then depends on his potential choice to interact or not, along with his capability to control them according to his volition. But when there are no choices to interact or not interact and when the system itself resists his volition, then he suffers a prisoner's fate. The system itself, in which he is caught, determines his potential freedom and choice. With the hope to survive he gives up his volition and adapts to the system's dictates.

Referring to the power of the man-made physical technological systems, Warren M. Brodey says:

We have accepted the proposition that in order to use the power which machines deliver economically, we must restrict ourselves to the limited human behaviors that the machines can accept as meaningful control. One must steer turning the steering wheel in the prescribed way regardless of one's body size, fatigue or personal style. Human behavior is mass produced by the power-delivering tools man has learned to depend on.[4]

The Framework: World-System
When the world is conceived of as a large-scale societal and political system, composed of ecological, social, economic, political and cultural subsystems, then the urban systems — upon which we are focussing in the following chapters — can be considered as small-scale subsystems similar to the larger systems. Both systems and subsystems show symptoms of immense *disintegration*, polarization, isolation and separation of their components. The world system shows contradictions and conflicts which are becoming immense in

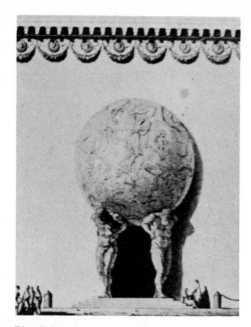

The disintegration of world systems: Millions for armaments, wars, moonshots, affluence and decadence — While 27,000 people starve every day

— the "economy of death."[5] They spend millions for armaments, wars and moon shots. They suffer from affluence, inflations and decadent social structures, while sixty per cent of the world's population goes unfed and 27,000 people starve to death every day.

The developing countries are steered and held together within the "stable" whole system through the power structure of the dominating super-nations. The latter as a rich minority oppress and exploit the poor underdeveloped majority of the world, bringing them wars, bloody or economic, to force adaptation to their system.

This power stability of the unequal world system, however, is seriously threatened by:

— Armies of revolutionaries generated by hunger, poverty and underemployment throughout the world.

— The information catastrophe, an avalanche of isolated and unstructured information which can be even partly processed only by the super-nations.

— The growing reaction to manipulation of individuals heightened by alienation, over-consumption and automation.

— The ecological catastrophe caused by lack of technological foresight, the abdication of human responsibility and uncontrolled concentrations of people,

their dimensions. There are a few power-holding countries, possessing four-fifths of the world's wealth, clinging to their beliefs in pure economic growth and technological advancement

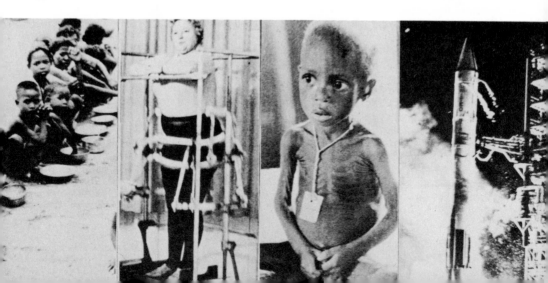

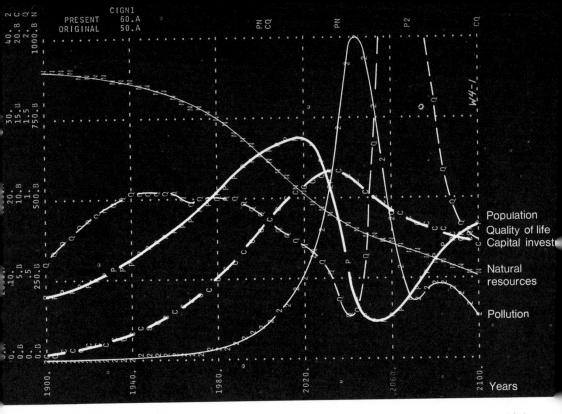

Population
Quality of life
Capital invest
Natural
resources
Pollution

Years

*Computed world catastrophe without
interventions*

industry, information, technology and
capital.

The super-nations are responding to
these threats with long-range planning
for future interventions to keep the
world system stable in their economic
interest. New methods are required to
conceive the world system politically
and economically as a complex whole
and to predict scientifically the complex
consequences of long-range decisions
(*social feedforward instrument*). From
Buckminster Fuller we learn how to
establish the base of the new methods.
Within his "world game"[6] he traces and
plans the present available technical
and natural resources in the whole
world, while neglecting the political
realities. *"Scenarios"* on *"dymaxion*

world maps" are the basis upon which
to determine the required energy for
food, clothing, communication, travel,
housing, disposal and so on, for the
year 2000. According to technocratic
reason (rationality), various energy
sources can be equally distributed on
the maps. Then, computing the scenarios one can find out, for example, that
by equal distribution more than enough
energy and resources for the survival of
the entire world would be available. But,
going back into the political reality of
U.S. imperialism (the steering system),
we can assume that this vision will
never be realized, and that instead the
"world game" in the hands of politicians
and economists will be simply misused
as a more sophisticated method to continue with the unequal distribution, exploitation of dependent countries and
realization of powerful interests. Buckminster Fuller's innovation of the geo-

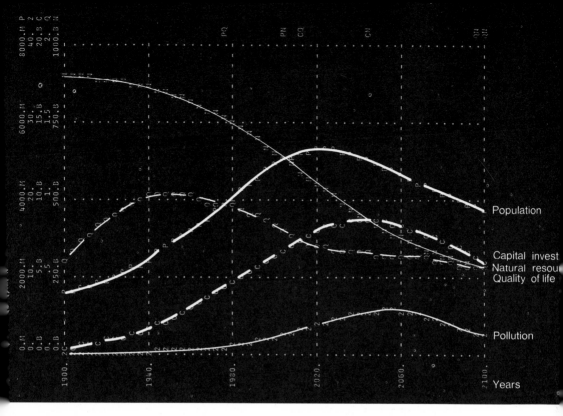

Population

Capital invest
Natural resou
Quality of life

Pollution

Years

desic dome and its subsequent use in the war industry is a harbinger.

"World Dynamics,"[7] on the other hand, an advanced method "not to predict the future but to identify what factors in the world situation are critical in determining the long-term evolution of civilization," is already developed, headed by Jay W. Forrester and commissioned by the Club of Rome. Global problems can be fed into a feedback computer model, attacking the problems according to the nation's pure economic interests, reflected in the choice of the following variables that are assumed to be controllable: world population; capital investment in industry; capital investment in food production; the world inventory of natural resources and the level of man's interference with nature, notably pollution.

By continuing the present politics of the "golden age" Forrester then pre-

Computed world catastrophe avoided through system-rational interventions and oppressive politics

dicts with his model a world catastrophe caused by a world-industrialization and urbanization. With fascistic overtones, he therefore proposes a more effective oppression of the developing countries to prevent their increasing populations, increasing demands for food, shelter, energy and industrialization, and their potential contribution to environmental pollution. Only then might the advanced countries keep their high living standards while "the present underdeveloped countries may be in a better condition for surviving the forthcoming worldwide environmental and economic pressure than are the advanced countries."[8] This proposal shows clearly the new technocrato-fascism rising within these new model

39

approaches to justify world-wide interventions by the super-nations.

However, those efforts to steer and to adapt the world with western technocratic comprehensive knowledge and *system-rational interventions* seem to result more from the agony of the power-holder than from real threats of the oppressed world.

However, unpredictable events and the increasing contradiction, inherent in the world system, will threaten its stability with violent conflicts. Latin America's population is predicted to rise during the next thirty years to 650 million people,[9] thereby aggravating already oppressive living conditions and adding impetus to already existing revolutionary movements. Africa's new nations are entangled in civil wars that are effacing boundaries set by colonial powers; and the people of Asia, even though they are starving, are beginning to engage in a collective uprising. If this trend continues revolutionary forces and countries of the Third World are likely to determine what happens within the world system of the future, rather than the present powerholders.

Social Systems

When societal models are conceived as systems, they can be seen to show many different attributes. *Political scientists* name them "highly complex, non-determined, relatively isolated systems;" mathematicians say that "they are characterized by the size of their lattices, and number of their properties and relations;" and the economists call them "complex systems which refer to a high-order, multiple-loop and non-linear feedback structure."[10]

The *social scientists* differentiate more detailed models:[11]

1. The *mechanical model*[12] of society is defined as a relatively closed system with almost no openings and links to the environment, with a continuity of self-perpetuation and with a maintenance of an "equilibrium." Punishments and sanctions link the different component elements together and neutralize internal basic contradictions. Only external threats can cause internal disturbances as internal self-regulation or adaptation is impossible.

2. The *organic model* is defined as a preeminently cooperative flexible system with different principles of organization between individual and collective elements. It has self-regulating capabilities and it maintains its equilibrium and structure despite internal and external changes and contradictions. It regulates by neutralizing arising conflicts.

3. The *process model* is defined as an adaptive, complex, open system with openings and links to its environment and with multi-faceted and fluid interplay of associations and disassociations in widely varying degrees and intensities. Its system structure is adaptive. Internal, external and interactive dialectical processes continually change its elements and the system as a whole. Capitalistic societies, for example, work according to a process model. Only optimum level of *stability* and *adaptive dynamic* can balance the antagonisms.

The Social System and Its Environment

External (environmental) or internal changes in the social system cause continual basic tensions within the system and towards the environment. Surpluses or lack of information, irregularities, deviation and contradictory processes and goals must be neutralized through the system itself. It needs *system-autonomy* to balance itself into an *optimal level system,* according to its goals and objectives. The most influential factors in achieving this balance are the flexibility of its parts, its control over the openness of its boundaries and its structural adaptability. With the loss of system autonomy, the system will be dissolved through adaptive or destructive pressures and environmental interventions.

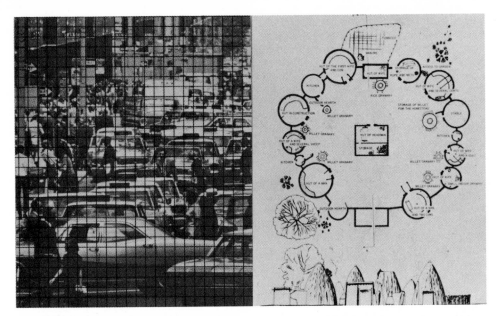

The open society versus the romantic image of the closed society

Steering the behavior of complex social systems, therefore, is a double interacting problem. It demands the knowledge of how to steer, operate and measure actions, reactions and resources *within* the internal system itself, as well as how to process and steer those happening in the external environment. A selective mechanism is needed to reduce and filter out the environmental and internal complexity and variability according to the internal system-structure, system-functions and order of goals and objectives. Only then can effective *system-rational decisions* be made, i.e. whether to adapt to its environment, stabilize its own structure or do both.

A rivalry of interests between the *system* and its *environment* involves questions of control, intervention and adaptation. Neither can achieve full control of the other without extensive

The mechanical regulator

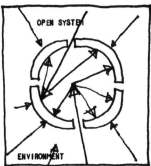
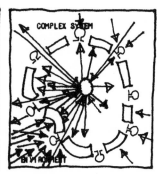

41

information about the other's structure, function and decision processes. Selective, communicative components from each must be exchanged into the opponent's system. Within the political context, for example, the necessary information exchange is expected to take place between institutions and people through public control, public hearings and citizen participation. The administrative systems and institutions, however, are too sealed up, closed and inflexible. The sporadic integration of citizens only fulfills the purpose of one-way communication: namely, developing adaptive environmental strategies, maximizing the system's information about its environment rather than as outside control through the environment.

Self-Organizing Systems
From cybernetics we learn how to create a single interactive mechanism to correct system steering and external and internal information selection with a set of decisions, controls and goals. Systems can be equipped with internal and external *regulators* or *sensory receptors* which receive, filter and select flows of energy and information which are subject to constant fluctuations. To avoid useless and disturbing information or energy, certain optimized limits for deviations must be set within the regulators and adjusted according to given system goals. *Low entropy*[13] (as in a mechanical system) makes adjustments easily, while *high entropy* (open complex system) requires experiments to determine the optima (the trial-and-error method). Deviations in internal as well as external information flows are compared with the given *system goals.* Necessary corrections are given to a steering-, correction- or *policy-mechanism* which initiates changes until the regulator receives sufficient information. This feedback[14] circle as a whole repeats with every relevant deviation. If

the system reacts, corrects itself, succeeds and adapts according to self-given performance goals, the system is a *self-organizing* one.

Finally, complex social adaptive systems are self-organizing when they are able to control their input-output performances in relation to their goals and when they develop strategies for their survival, maintenance, expansion, growth, adaptation and defense against intervention and threats.

Urban Systems
Conceiving now urban environments as complex social systems, the medieval town presents itself as an integrated, relatively autonomous, non-adaptive, stable and closed system. Its coherent physical, economic, social and cultural components were tightly integrated into its function and structure. The social and physical parts of the system expressed themselves in all aspects of its life.

Inside, the church and salvation *vs. outside,* rejection and damnation.
Inside, order *vs. outside,* chaos.
Inside, security *vs. outside,* threat.
Inside, privacy *vs. outside,* community.
Inside, the house *vs. outside,* the streets and squares.

Relevant system-disturbances come only from the outside — the threatening militant environment.

On the other hand, present American cities are open, polarized, disintegrated, non-autonomous and dynamic systems, with invisible (but functional) boundaries and with numerous links to and dependencies on their environments. Actual threats are internal. They come from its antagonistic social and physical systems. Its inhabitants, conditioned to believe in success and prosperity, yield to aggression, competition and exploitation. Permanently controlled with enormous concentrations of political and economic power, they attempt to survive

The mediaeval city as a closed, cohesive and integrating system

---

amid ever increasing social and physical disintegration and contradictions.

In the era of monopoly capitalism a spontaneous dissolution of the large city takes place and intensifies the growth of suburbs. The fundamental components then become: the central city, the small satellite center (old and new) tending toward a certain optimum size, the workers' suburb, the factory town, the village and farm, the industrial complex, the research center, and the shopping center. Various institutions and services move away from the city: hotels, movies, stadiums, hospitals, schools, camps, etc. All these elements are linked by a single transportation and communication network. Together they constitute the megalopolis: the unplanned result of urban growth under contemporary capitalism.[15]

It is the abstract, capitalist "system"[16] which institutes and allows urban interventions based on contradictory and partial problem-thinking. Accordingly, urban solutions frequently contradict and exclude each other. There are one-dimensional interventions of the human-hostile power structures standing behind the urban processes. The unlimited development of technology combined with the explosion of population generating uncontrolled expansion of cities will continually bring about an overwhelming new and unexpected set of social problems. And we can assume that coming capitalistic solutions will be the same: fragmentary, partial and one-dimensional profit-oriented solutions unrelated to local and human problems, yet expanded to new dimensions and with far-reaching social consequences.

The chaos and urban exhaustion is already evident in the social and physical cuttings, divisions, partitions, segregations and isolations. So it is hard to

Left: The present American system

interpret this kind of city as a *complex developing adaptive social system.* It is more a conglomeration, accumulation, one-upon-beside-under-over-against-another of simple and complex physical, economic, organizational, technical and social, independent, isolated and contradictory systems. These systems are adaptive to the irrational dominating system of capitalism, and not, as they should be, adaptive to people and needs which they determine. The capitalist urban systems are systems that serve and are dominated by the interests of the power elites instead of by those of the people. Consequently interventions concern only the generation and maintenance of profit-oriented urban function (networks of private transportation, the business centers, the administrative palaces, the government centers, boring high-rental residential areas). Even petitioning for political power to set limits to the urban exploitation in behalf of the threatened people does not help, as the politicians, caught within ideological blinders, have no farsighted ideas for

Top and bottom: Scenes of spontaneous dissolution and "one-dimensional" ad-hoc interventions

harvard,

CAMBRIDGE 1869

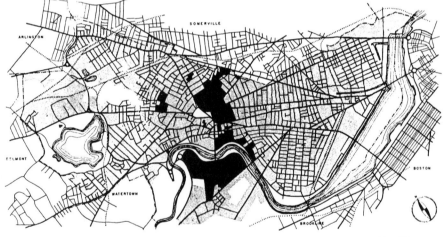

☐ DEVELOPED AREA ■ HARVARD UNIVERSITY CAMBRIDGE 1969

urban
imperialist

solutions to establish new urban systems. They even participate in the profitable interfering business world, so they reduce their efforts to occasional irrelevant warnings that sound good. How can something change if the physician does not recognize that he in his profession is the one who is sick? It needs revolutionary intervention!

And, as Alex Tzonis says:

It is the class of people versus the class of fetishes, the formalistic objects, the technological gadgets, the bureaucratic institutions. The alienated city of the fetishes grows and drains the human every day . . . The acceptance of the desires and goals of the system that recognizes a single individual and his values as the client-decision maker of the environment has resulted in the disintegration of human contact within our man-made environment.[17]

The Self-Organizing Chaos

The conservative urban planner likes to maintain that the city is an organic social model as opposed to a centralized mechanistic model. Although the concept of self-organizing systems can be applied to single enterprises, organizations and some political and economic subsystems, it is difficult to apply these criteria to present whole cities — the parts and the whole show completely different behaviors. That the parts are isolated, exhausted and anarchistically related is obvious and is a result inherent to the concepts of darwinian "competition" and the "free enterprise system."

The city-as-whole cannot survive by itself.[18] It needs all kinds of outside support, as from centralized government programs. It does not seem to be in control of its inputs, outputs, inner mechanisms or anything else. There are control-mechanisms only within the conditional and economic subsystems (e.g., the subsystem "law and order" or the money-market subsystem); systems necessary to maintain capitalism's system-stability. Other subsystems, especially the social ones, have no built-in performance controls.

In order to create a city which would be "self-organizing" according to active criteria, one would have to consider the following actions: first, changing all existing systems and subsystems into so-called feedback structures in order to establish appropriate measures for their actual performance. Profits and "law and order" as performance measures are only applicable to a few systems; most are measured differently (education values, communication values, etc.). Regulators would take the form of a network of newly established publicly controlled institutions representing the opinions and needs of the population. These *base-institutions* would have to be given open constitutions, open accessibilities and power to direct effective interventions. Since these institutions themselves would be the parameters, adjustment of the regulators would not be necessary. Political institutions for urban affairs (*urban intelligence centers*)[19] would derive information and sets of goals from the regulators. Decisions and correcting actions would be controlled by the base-institutions, representing the basic needs of society.

But the "self-organizing" city remains within capitalism an illusion. Firstly, cybernetics for urban problems is still in its beginnings and, secondly, powerful free public institutions would threaten the system of capitalism. Capitalism needs the maintenance of firm boundaries, in the form of strong and clear separations as a means of political and social power.

Classes, races, professions, class-oriented education, property, status, man, woman, rich, poor, homosexual, heterosexual, sane, insane etc. are some of the social expressions; and suburbs, slums, prisons, capitols, banks etc. are

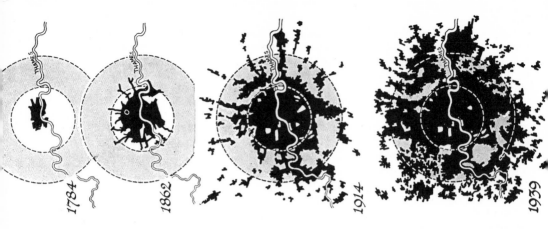

Uncontrolled "natural growth" of cities

some of the physical expressions of separation and limitation of subsystems. The systems' decision-makers do not want to break down these divisions through the establishment of public institutions. They prefer to go along using remote scientific methods, deceitful manipulation and infiltration and indirect interventions into the citizens' lives to achieve the acceptance of the present inhuman urban conditions as given.

Controlled growth — Washington D.C. decentralized (L. Hilbersheimer)

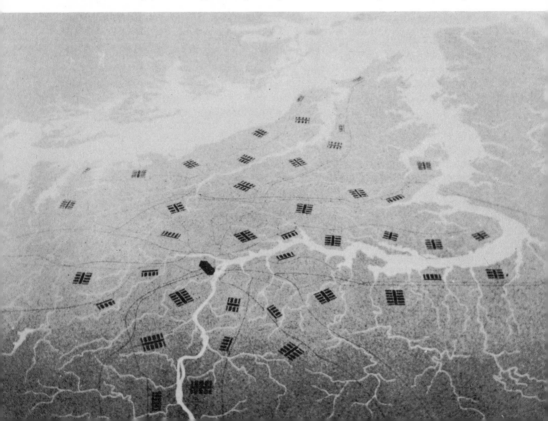

V. QUALITATIVE ANALYSIS

One way to understand more fully the urban systems in their comprehensive social and political context is to discuss critically the framework of "value-free" scientific urban qualitative and quantitative systems analysis along with their applications and consequences.

Qualitative systems analysis gives insight primarily into formal, functional and structural relationships between system components of given systems, rather than into quantitative facts and efficiencies.

Normative and empirical sciences provide the means to reduce system complexities into models of logical interdependent relationships. This is done by *breaking* the *complex system* into *perceivable subsystems* and *part problems*.

Early *structural-analytical* attempts to develop a conceptual understanding of urban systems, their organizational principles and complexities, were made by the architect and mathematician, Christopher Alexander. He introduced the concepts of *semi-lattice*[1] and *tree structures*[2] into planning and urban analysis. Assuming a reciprocity between the urban-social and the urban-physical structures, he maintained that the "natural city" (e.g. Vienna, Liverpool, Manhattan) during its origin and growth

is a combination of social tree structures and functional physical semi-lattice structures. The highly organized social structures are flexible enough to overlap continuously and simultaneously with the less ordered functional physical structures. The "artificial city" (Levittown, Brasilia, Chandigarh) is, in contrast, a combination of social semi-lattice structures (he refers to the concept of the "open society") and of physical tree structures (the clearly defined environmental boundaries).

C. Alexander severely criticizes the existence and the increasing use of "inhuman" and boring tree structures in constructing urban environments. He concludes that separation, segregation and disassociation within the urban environment are the results of tree structures. "If we make cities which are trees, they will cut our life within to pieces."[3]

The fascinating thing in this analysis is Alexander's concept of the semi-lattice; the questionable half-truth, however, is his conclusion. For both types of cities are generated by the same society: a capitalistic society which has priorities of efficiency and exploitation and which is *functionally closed* but *structurally open*. That means that life in Manhattan's semi-lattices, mostly the product of *laissez-faire* capitalism, is no alternative to Levittown's trees and mono-society, the product of late capitalism. Both solutions are integrated into the system of capitalism, a "system" that absorbs every formal structure if economic efficiency is guaranteed. It is

---

Life in Manhattan's threatening semi-lattices is no alternative to Levittown's trees and monosociety

Top: The naturally grown city
Bottom: The artificially planned city

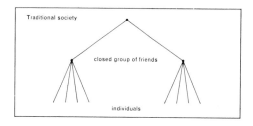

Traditional society

closed group of friends

individuals

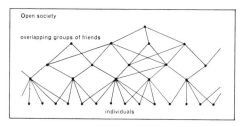

Open society

overlapping groups of friends

individuals

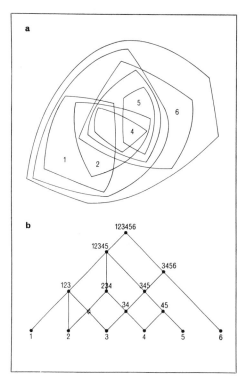

a

5

6

4

1

2

b

123456

12345

3456

123   234   345

34   45

1   2   3   4   5   6

Semi-lattices

this system that cuts people into pieces.

To understand *urban-social, -organizational* and *-industrial* systems in the broadest sense, however, we must use a more thorough-going approach. The methods of general systems analysis and organizational systems analysis can be helpful here. These methods use and manipulate a set of system parameters and variables in order to discover the principles of the system under study. Some of these parameters and variables are the following:

System rationality is a principle which eliminates irrational transcendental behaviors, generates system alternatives and simplifies, neutralizes and de-emotionalizes.[4]

Purposive rational systems-behavior (as defined by Habermas) produces the choice of appropriate means for reaching certain goals (instrumental action) and the rational choice of alternative goals (strategic action).

System purposes are responses to existing scarcities. If systems are not equipped to satisfy all given demands and achieve all given goals at once, the system elements must be subordinated to one order of priorities and a generalized common purpose.

Organization of different *system-purposes* and *functions* avoids system-destructive internal neutralizations, contradictions and conflicts. Sequences and hierarchies of purposes coordinate the principle of rationalization; i.e., various purposes must be optimally balanced according to general system goals. A team of researchers, for example, is subject to the following possibly contradictory purposes: each member of the unit must exhibit initiative, independence and imaginative creativity. Most extraordinary solutions, however, are excluded by institutionalized censors. The research *system* creates a balance to produce innovative but acceptable solutions. Accordingly, the scope of system purposes determines the system functions; at this point, *purposive functions.* They essentially influence the systems' rationalization and flexibility.

System-specialization and *differentiation* when the number and complexity of problems to be solved surpasses the capabilities of the system functions and the system performances. The system must be divided into specialized subsystems with specified functions. Each part, generating specific optimizations, problem-solving processes and complex part performances, must somehow be integrated into a Whole.

Dividing systems into *cooperating* differentiated *subsystems* alone cannot increase total system performances. Simultaneous intensification of communication, organization and flexibility is needed. Since input-output relationships among subsystems must be carefully regulated, the total system becomes a dense net of relations and dependencies. There is reciprocity between system *quality* and *quantity:* the more differentiated the system, the further extended its performance. System complexity and system variability increase enormously. Each deviation, once detected and characterized, can be treated as an individual and localized problem. An exchange of elements does not affect the system as a whole.

To keep systems *operational* and manageable, a continual problem-solving process must be guaranteed. Similar problems are solved with equivalent solutions[5] to save time and reduce effort. Non-predictable by-problems, resulting from inflexible purposive system functions, may lead to open internal conflicts. These disturbances must be neutralized by appropriate functional or structural system changes.

Within social systems psychological methods are available; the neutralization of opposition, the isolation of individuals or groups; the concealment of problems by covering them up or making them more abstract. There are also the well-known traditional methods: hierarchical and formal oppression.

Example of a Qualitative Analysis

The planner-architect Richard J. Dietrich[6] developed a method of describing complex social systems based on *development parameters* which compare the quality of different systems and determine system performances in different states and at different moments, similar to the method of cultural anthropology. The parameters are:

1. The grade of differentiation: a measure of differentiation, specialization and individuality.

2. The grade of variability: a measure of capability for change, regeneration

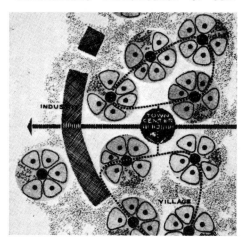

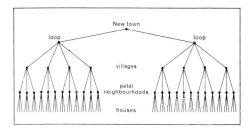

Tree-structures

and adaptation of the system states.

3. The grade of communication: a measure of the intensity of the interactions of material and informational exchanges among the system elements.

4. The grade of complexity: a measure of the complexity of the network, the density and the dependency of the system elements.

5. The grade of organization: a measure of the organization of the system elements.

A general *optimal* system state, called an *"integral level,"* is achieved when a system reaches an optimal functioning or performance level at a certain degree of development, having minimized performance expenditures (input) and maximized system performance (output). Each measurement must relate to a specific set of environmental influences which change through time.

An optimal developing system within this context means the change from one "integral level" to another one of higher quality. Single elements can develop and adapt at different speeds. If great differences appear, the system reaches a *"disintegral phase"* in which either the other elements catch up with the higher element level or the total system ends its "life" as a whole. In the latter case single parts develop their *own dynamics.*

Applying these parameters, Dietrich analyzes levels and historical developments of various social and urban systems. Within his approach he makes it clear that the present societal *subsystem "communication"* — which involves the exchange of energy, information and material — is the actual agent for social systems' development. For example, the phenomenon of warfare: part of the subsystem communication produced most technical inventions later used in other subsystems. Weapons were among the first simple tools; the first atomic energy application was the bomb; and the first transistors served

military purposes; as do the geodesic domes and the think tank research companies like Rand. Other subsystems, under pressure to develop similar and supplementary reactions in order to catch up, follow more or less slowly the "progressive" subsystem communication.

Applying Dietrich's analysis to the present American urban society reveals the horrifying situation: exponentially growing disintegration of the whole system society reinforced by the power of the subsystem "communication." While we have fourth-generation computers, immense transportation systems, superdense energy provision, air transportation and space networks, overly-precise control and communication systems generated by huge differentiated industrial systems, there remains an underdeveloped social system of entangled class contradictions, open race conflicts and power elites — a situation that is deteriorating rather than improving.

Tensions between the single subsystems in America become so great that comprehension or optimization of the whole society is no longer possible. The control over the socio-technical system as a whole is lost. There remains a corporate techno-economic industrial and political subsystem manipulated by technocratic-political means.

This method of analysis — the description of parts and the whole and their reciprocity — is essentially valid within the development of qualitative analysis of social change. The results of its application to American society, however, seem to be oversimplified. Dietrich tries to formally analyze urban decay in relation to the total U.S. system. But, neglecting the actual agents behind the subsystem communication and the "disintegral phrases," he is unable to develop realistic system strategies for interventions to reach a new "integral phase." So he ignores the fact that the "system" of capitalism, remaining operational, *needs disintegration* and high

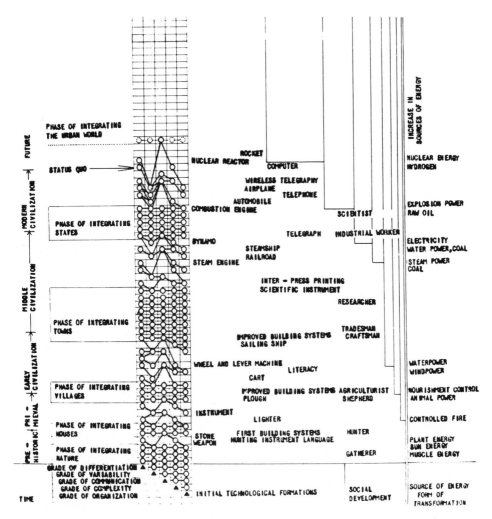

System development parameter applied to historical developments

tension between its subsystems. Its "system rationality" means social inequity and irrationality — inescapable consequences of its essential dynamic. Consequently, he naively proposes to govern the "system" to a new integral phase with technological means. Flexible, easily changeable, highly differentiated self-organizing subsystems, he says, should reunite people with the technical world, change the structural imperatives, stop the urban massacres and eliminate the power elites — the dream of all utopian technocrats. Dreams of a totally malleable world with totally liberated individuals. Dreams of a liberal paradise where people float through mental and real worlds without any resistance or conflict.

Despite these inadequacies this formal analysis does indicate that qualita-

tive analysis can be an excellent tool to reveal, criticize or question system purposes, functions, relations, contradictions, disfunctions and inhuman consequences in organized societies, industries, cities, factories and organizations. It can show clearly the developing tendencies of systems and can indicate destructive parts, subsystems or functions which are disintegrated and which disintegrate the people involved and concerned.

In general, to develop strategies for real and urgent change within the most rotten social subsystems, qualitative systems analysis might be appropriate to attack pollution as well as the U.S. courts, the systems of welfare, the system of unhealth and the systems of urban non-planning. This last, espe-cially, is highly socially disintegrated but "system" integrated: one-dimensional physical and economic planning, as opposed to *"social planning"* with technocratic planning in a subordinate role.

The technocrats, however, reject qualitative analysis as an instrument for understanding urban systems and a foundation for social change. They claim to alleviate the threatening population explosion exclusively with one-dimensional planning and *quantitative* systems analysis. They prepare for rationalized and functionalized systems. The hope and intention of the technocrat is clear: functionalized people will and can adapt to whatever structures he establishes.

Dreams of utopian technocrats

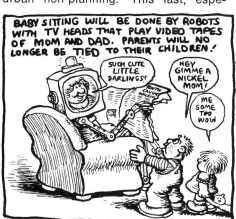

ONCE A YEAR ALL THE OLD STUFF WILL BE GATHERED UP AND PUT INTO HUGE MACHINES WHICH WILL GRIND IT UP AND MAKE IT INTO NEW STUFF!

THE BED AS WE KNOW IT WILL BE REPLACED BY A SOFT, WARM, MOIST FOAM PLASTIC BLOB THAT YOU JUST DIVE INTO AND FALL ASLEEP WHILE IT UNDULATES SLOWLY IN AND OUT AND SOOTHING, SWEET MUSIC PLAYS.

YOU WON'T HAVE TO SHIT ANYMORE! BOWELS WILL BE REMOVED AT BIRTH AND A SANITIZING DISPOSAL UNIT IN-STALLED. NEEDS EMPTYING ONLY ONCE A MONTH. NO MORE WORRY ABOUT SMELLY EXCREMENT! GOOD-BYE TOILET!!

BUILDINGS, CARS WILL BE SOFT PLASTIC. STREETS WILL BE SOFT PLASTIC. ACCIDENTS WILL BE A THING OF THE PAST. NOBODY WILL GET HURT ANYMORE!

EVERYONE WILL BE TUNED IN TO EVERY-THING THAT'S HAPPENING ALL THE TIME! NO-ONE WILL BE LEFT OUT. WE'LL ALL BE NORMAL!

NOBODY WILL WORK! ALL PRODUCTION, DISTRIBUTION AND MAINTENANCE WILL BE DONE BY COMPUTERIZED ROBOTS. PEOPLE CAN SPEND ALL OF THEIR TIME PLAYING, EATING, OR WATCHING TV!

VI. QUANTITATIVE ANALYSIS

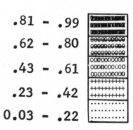

PROBABILITY
LEGEND

.81 - .99

.62 - .80

.43 - .61

.23 - .42

0.03 - .22

The quantitative analyses, or "urban models," are felt to be the long-expected breakthrough in developing complex problem descriptions and problem-solving processes for environmental and social steering techniques. They have become the technocrats' instruments for realizing their dreams of large-scale rationalized planning for *urban interventions,* and their premises for the fast, economic yet profitable mass-production and change of cities. Their interests no longer focus on a freely developing anarchistic *project-oriented* production of urban environments. Instead, with their quantitative analysis, they orient themselves to *developing-processes* within the swiftly growing and changing cities and to technocratic politics (push-button politics) for effective *functional* and *balanced* interventions.

In contrast to the method of qualitative analysis, the complexities to be broken into subsystems and subproblems are disentangled mostly with the methods of natural normative sciences. Based on the application of symbolic and mathematical logic to the description of the relationships between the systems' parameters and variables, numerous mathematical models already have been developed. They are supposed to represent qualities, quantities, components, problems, laws, principles and theories of the urban environments. The computer models are then manipu-

Output of a predictive model — Map showing the spatial distributions of probabilities that land will be developed

lated and used as instruments for the development, repetition, projection and comparison of principles, laws and theories. Since they consist of systems of up to 10,000 equations, they must be precise and internally consistent *without logical errors.*

Models can be classified generally, as Robert Boguslaw[1] does:
1. The *formalistic* (formal and analytical) models which manipulate known variables to form models of known and established situations.
2. The *heuristic* models based on the manipulation of solutions derived from equivalent solutions.
3. The *operational* models manipulated according to predetermined goals to be achieved.
4. The *ad hoc* models applied to situations where no prepared analysis exists, where different and changing conditions and purposes cause a situation within the future to be unknown and undefined, where problems of implementation arise or where continuous small changes are to be implemented with immediate effectiveness by maintaining the basic structure of the given situation.

Unfortunately, most existing *urban models* belong to the category of *ad hoc models.* Their given purpose is to achieve and test interim stages and compromises following the current trends. Whatever modelling data and means happen to be available are taken as satisfying vital needs, without questioning them or relating them to a broader context. The consequences are obvious: perpetuation of and adaptation to the given situation with all its irrational reflections of contemporary concepts, conditions, technologies and fashions; a corresponding inability to innovate, to create new forms or to make long-range predictions and a trend toward continual application and development of the same models, based on immediate usefulness, effectiveness and ease of application and economy.

Urban *ad hoc* models can be classified more specifically: according to the situations to be modelled (relocation of retail markets, location of industry, housing, growth of cities), according to model construction theory and methods (gravitation and feedback theory), or according to the model function and purpose (description, prediction, planning, simulation, evaluation, distribution, allocation).

Ira S. Lowry[2] distinguishes between three categories of urban models:

The descriptive models (social feedback instruments)[3] which "reveal much about the structure of the urban environment, reducing the apparent complexity of the observed world to the coherent and rigorous language of mathematical rela tionships."

The predictive models (social feedfor· ward instruments)[4] for the prediction of the future. "If one is able to postulate the direction of causation, knowledge of the future value of the 'cause' enables one to predict the future value of the effect."

The planning models which "necessarily incorporate the method of conditional prediction, but they go further in that outcomes are evaluated in terms of the planning goals."

Each of these models is supposed to represent, evaluate or describe a limited urban environment and its activities through "a set of symbolic representations of relationships."[5] The task is accomplished by "abstracting urban phe-

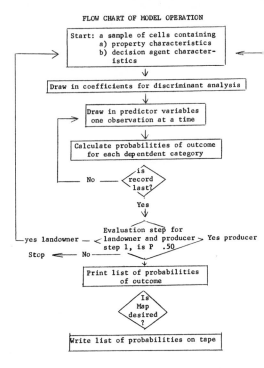

FLOW CHART OF MODEL OPERATION

Note: the landowner and producer recycling is to move the landowner parcels into the developer stage, and the developer step 1 observations into step 2.

Flow chart of a predictive model

nomena to symbolic form and relating those in a structural and mathematical operational way." Once the model is created, random observations and working hypotheses can be recapitulated in symbolic terms. They will be proved or rejected according to the model's reaction. Additionally, it can be used as a prediction, projection and decision instrument to test consequences, alternatives, policies and plans being considered. Accordingly, urban experiments can be made in "urban laboratories" instead of in real situations.

The *planning models*[6] and the *development of planning theory,* however, are seen as more complex. They are differentiated into and composed of a

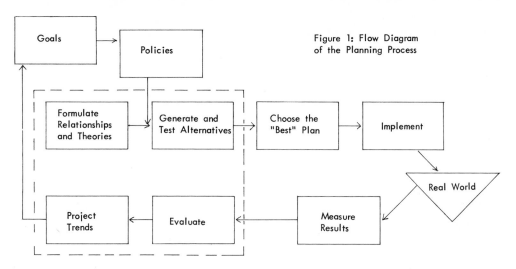

Figure 1: Flow Diagram of the Planning Process

Program		Time	Cost	Technology
1(a)	Justification	L	H	L
1(b)	Staffing and organizing	M	M	L
1(c.1)	Persuasion	M-H	M	M
1(c.2)	Education	M-H	M	M
1(c.3)	Politics	M-H	M	L
1(d)	Implementation	H	M	M
2(a)	Decision maker	L	M	L
2(b)	Alternatives	H	L	M
2(c)	Goals	M	H	M
2(d)	Objectives	M	H	M
2(e)	Effectiveness (alternatives)	M	M	H
2(f)	Effectiveness (goals)	M	M	L
2(g)	Optimal	L	M	H
3(a)	Simulation	L	M	H
3(b)	Counterplanning	M	M	M
3(c)	Control	M	M	M

Planning models — Differentiation and composition into various stages and submodels

---

number of stages and submodels: the establishment of a system of planning goals, the design of alternatives, the prediction of alternatives, the choice of the best alternative, the implementation (realization). Rationalization, formalization and standardization of the different planning steps and decisions becomes necessary to formulate each stage as a separate submodel, to link together and to compare all the parts of the whole planning process. The application and methodology of existing and new urban models thereby assumes a functional significance in shaping new planning methods, models and theories.

Generally, the role of the *first generation* of urban models is to provide a social feedback instrument which, however, is restricted and limited. As Maurice Kilbridge says:

Analytical methods and particularly symbolic models, can assist greatly in the development of theory. We believe that this is the major role of urban models today. We suggest that their secondary role is to help policy makers sharpen their judgment through more explicit statement of assumptions and consequences of alternative means, thereby limiting subjectivity in selection from among alternative policies and programs.[7]

Within the development of the *second generation,* however, the secondary role becomes the primary one. The model is less an instrument for theory development than for policy decisions. As a policy-making social feedforward instrument, the actual power of the model is evident in its conceptual clarity and economic technical rationality. It builds an empirical systematic framework for deductions and inductions of urban theories and policies.

However, reviewing and analyzing the existing urban models and focusing on given preconditions, basic assumptions and the consequences of applications, we deduce that actually these rational expectations are based on pretentions, irrationalities and questionable ideologies.

Preconditions of the Modelling Process

Since the limitations — where the model is to be applied, its purpose and goals — must be determined before the modelling process starts, scientific, economic and political predecisions underlie the entire planning process. The first silent integration of capitalistic ideologies and irrationalities occurs through the circumstances of scientific competition, funding dependencies and individual expectations as they develop in each of the researchers, the model builders and model commissioners. The predecisions then are accepted as structural imperatives and neutralized within the technocratic and pragmatic planning approaches. Being political and economic constraints, they are determined neither by a given human system nor by the realm of necessity. Thus the research result is roughly and deliberately defined even before the actual model process begins.

Consequently, the technocratic urban models concentrate on fragmented and profit-oriented selected aspects of urban activities: distribution of land-use and population, allocation of industries, housing and transportation. Developments for urban leisure time, recreation or health do not exist.

The urban models are either small-scale or of such narrow-gauged purpose that they do not begin to meet the vital need for complex urban problem description, problem solutions and developments of theories. Their actual use is more to rationalize, formalize and economize the given planning processes, to adapt urban activities as

rationally as possible and to reduce them as much as possible to economic efficiencies.[8] Thus, the application of these models to urban problems integrates urban activities into the realm of necessity and separates them from the realm of freedom. The consequent oppressive effects are clear.

Some Basic Assumptions

All models reflect basic assumptions within their definitions of urban activity and within their choices of which aspects of an urban situation are primary, which are secondary and so on. D. Seidman, for example, defines an urban activity as "any set locating entities such as households or retail employees."[9] James Hester describes five basic categories of activities and corresponding classifications of models based on each activity:[10]

1. *Aggregate growth driven by forces within the city.* The models analyze statistics of historical growth — increase in population, employment and industries, migration, births and deaths — and they give predictions of attraction and stimulation, location and redistribution of activities, changes or maintenance of structural framework.

2. *Internal shifts among the different social classes of the same activities.* (The "filtering process" by which upper income housing passes through several intermediate stages to become slum housing is one example of internal shifts.) Models use economic and statistical data to describe and predict these shifts.

3. *Location of activities within the city.* Models based on observed behavioral parameters, linear programming, regression analysis, optimization, stochastic and econometric models allocate manufacturing employment, retail employment or residential areas.

4. *Growth in the supply of space within the city.* (Growth occurs either through

expansion or increased building heights.) This kind of model "determines the spatial extent of an area that a city can cover and still support itself and maintain minimum levels of communication between its parts" by calculating long term trends, shifts in the distribution of activities and requirements for growth.

5. *Aggregate growth of activities driven by forces outside the city.* These models include federal programs and industrial development in neighboring cities.

The most striking point in these analyses of urban activities is not their simplification as much as their irrational and ideological choice of priorities. Only functional economic activities appear; the human-oriented ones are consciously left out. Of course, urban model builders give "scientific" justification for these omissions. They argue that human related needs and behavior are unpredictable, continuously changing and self-dynamic. They therefore are too difficult to include in the models.[11, 12] But when we consider the advances in social sciences and the knowledge and technical achievements shown by the industries based on need arousal, then we understand that the given "scientific" reasons reflect pure capitalistic priorities and that they scientifically are not necessarily true.

There are tacit agreements which allow that on one side unverified theories, irrational assumptions and complex economic relationships can be integrated and quantified into the rational model construction without question or consideration, while on the other side social and human factors are excluded under the pretension of being too complex and intractable to analytic techniques. Moreover, aspects based on distances, number of households, jobs or cars are included as *parameters* and *variables* simply because their values can be easily derived from statistics and economics and because they remain constant (or at least increase or decrease linearly) over time. Seidman, whose models are based on such easy quantifiable but limited aspects, states in self-justification that "predictive models are most accurate when the values of their parameters remain constant over time."[13]

Both these facts result in the simple determination and prediction of quantities, while qualitative present and future collective and individual needs given by the social reality are ignored. And while quantitative predictions of short-range consequences are highly probable and reliable, theory development is almost impossible and restricted to specified economic and statistical problems. Consequently, quantitative models encourage both the uncritical acceptance of the restricting preconditions and irrationalities, and the elimination of qualitative problems which are made to disappear among the dominating quantities.

As already mentioned, the justification of neglecting qualitative needs lies in the predecisions and construction of the models themselves. Finally, for the experts who apply them, nothing seems to be questionable. Fatal consequences can be seen, especially in the field of transportation where highway programs based on quantitative models meet the need for better and "faster" individual transportation, increased production, consumption and profits, but simultaneously neglect the impact of cars on people, pollution, space and the interventional destruction of the urban environment.

Following pages:

Flow chart of a transportation planning model

Transportation models — Side effects not taken into consideration and excluded as variables

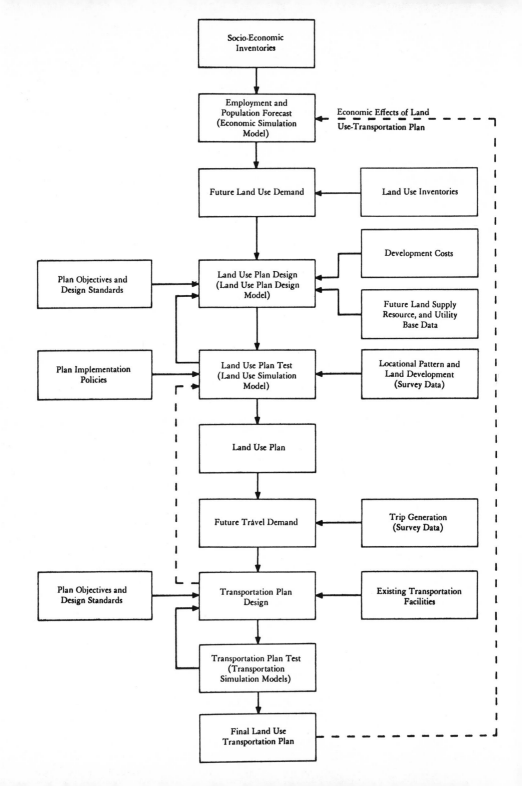

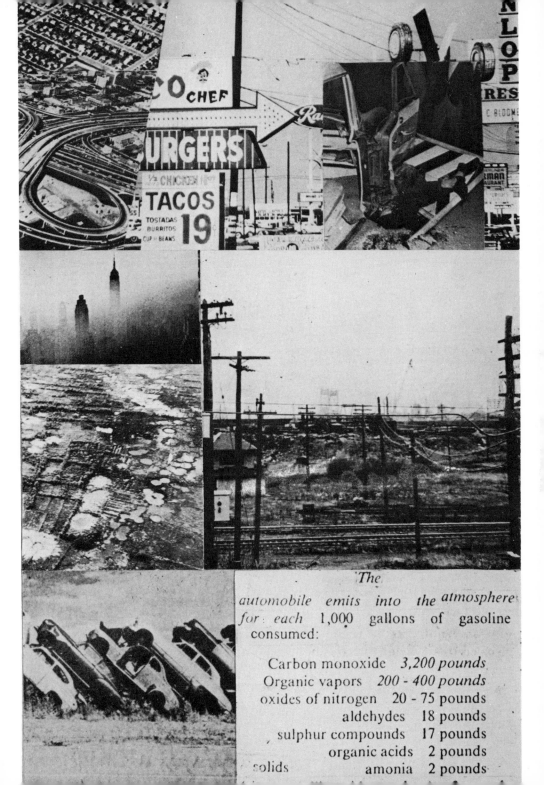

The automobile emits into the atmosphere for each 1,000 gallons of gasoline consumed:

Carbon monoxide   3,200 pounds
Organic vapors   200 - 400 pounds
oxides of nitrogen   20 - 75 pounds
aldehydes   18 pounds
sulphur compounds   17 pounds
organic acids   2 pounds
solids   amonia   2 pounds

City models which integrate all urban activity into a "total model" do not exist. Attempts to connect the various existing models of different activities by interpolation or sequential additions have not been successful. The lack of success mostly results from social conditions as scientific competition, individualism, fragmentation and lack of scientific planning. The existing part models are individually and differently constructed and can hardly be compared or added. Current computer capacities are not high enough. However, circumstantial and problem-distorting techniques for sequential computing of the "submodels" are in use.

Composing models is a process of abstraction and reduction of scope and complexity. Maurice Kilbridge proposes to do this in several stages:[14]

1. The formulation of a *comprehensive theory* of how urban systems operate, based on institutional knowledge about economic, physical and social relationships in cities.
2. The development of a *manageable theory.* This is done by narrowing the general theories in scope and dropping illogical, irrational and uncertain elements, transferring qualitative statements into quantitative ones and eliminating non-transferable qualities which concern social and technological elements.
3. Formulating the *remaining factors,* statements and elements explicitly within a logical framework of *mathematical equations.* Excessively complex ones must be simplified or even dropped.
4. Conversion of the equations into an appropriate *computer language,* considering computational constraints, available data banks and the economy of parameters and variables.

This method shows the actual problem with the models: necessary rationalism is distorted through predetermined and enforced irrationalities which in-

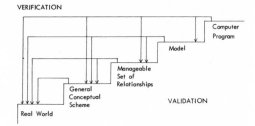

Figure 4: Verification and Validation
Work Down the Levels of Abstraction

trude into the model during the process of abstraction and simplification. Qualitative and comprehensive statements, even if they are developed in Stage 1, are considered too "soft" for the simulation and computing processes and are eliminated in Stage 2. At each succeeding stage more complexities are eliminated according to the model-builder's value system, the structural imperative and available computer technologies. In addition, objects under study must be isolated, i.e. existing connections or dependencies not correlated intensively with the object must be neglected and divided into *endogenous* variables and factors which can be manipulated within the model, and *exogenous* ones which influence it from the outside. The subtle process is not merely a rational simplification necessary to deal with a complex system at all but also an irrational imperative to repress specific methodological and substantial problems.

Additional problems within the modelling process are technical, economic and data-oriented — calibration, sensitivity and prediction tests and the accidental available data, usually unstructured or obsolete — which further distort the model in an irrational way. Overprecision and abundance, where they are not necessary, and over-generalization and lack of data, where they are needed, are generally accepted dilemmas attributed to either the difficulty of structuring the abundant resources or to costliness of acquiring additional data.

Therefore, one must realize that this process of decomposing or breaking a system into subsystems and subproblems, of evaluating the influence of exogenous variables and of determining endogenous parameters is based on a *subjective* interpretation of qualitative interrelationships formed into quantitative equations. Although subjectivity is necessarily involved because the planning subject is always part of the planning system itself, the danger of model building lies in the proposition that the planner, by using the systems approach, creates a "rational" model, thus not making clear the dominance of the input assumptions in comparison to the rational methods applied thereafter.

Experiments

An experiment with models differs from verification and implementation of hypotheses in so far as it is still considered part of the modelling process. Experiments should verify the model's logic itself, its simplified reflection of reality and its capacity to predict. To do this, historical data predicting historical events are in use. As far as one deals with theoretical *research* and *simulation models,* it is quite a useful way. *Operational models,* however, require real experiments, and in their case, the implementation of planning action must be used as an experiment. This provokes an old dilemma: the division between theory and practice. In physics or in pure science one deals with abstract concepts and inanimate objects. If experiments fail, one can start again. Experiments with operational urban models, however, affect people and intervene into their lives. And, considering the *irreversibility* of urban processes and their adaptation imperatives, they cannot be repeated. Mistakes become facts and cannot simply be cancelled. On the other hand, the application of prediction and simulation models brings little hope. Since these are based on *probabilities* (usually probabilistic models) and on processable quantities, they are not reliable in terms of any quality.

Even so, the model designer seems not to worry about the implications of his work. He is, in reality, dealing with subjects and qualities and not merely objects and quantities, although the two are interdependent and indivisible. Boguslaw says: "the new utopians are concerned with nonpeople and with people-substitutes."[15]

Finally, tests, evaluations and predictions of alternatives can be considered as experiments, even when their character is only slightly experimental. The model constructions and computer technologies, however, are limited to alternatives which reflect and extend the present social capitalistic conditions. Real contrary alternatives, including qualitative social and environmental change, would explode the model frameworks. They cannot be included in tests or integrated into the new planning approaches. They do not fit into the "test-evaluation-prediction-machines," which are composed for and operated with only specific kinds of capitalistic ideas.

Some model builders, aware of the weaknesses and limitations of the models, consider the whole modelling approach an experiment, perhaps in order to prevent criticism. This solution is naive, as the models will be applied as soon as possible, considering the huge investments made in them. Any model conception or plan, either bad or good, made by influential research teams is part of reality, forms the thinking of the model builders through learning, criticism and reworking and influences the trend of scientific advance. In this way the model concepts increase the "power of scientific organization"[16] and of social adaptation to maintain the system's stability. They change our

Ninths of Development

■	9
▓	7 - 8
▨	5 - 6
▒	3 - 4
░	1 - 2
□	0

LAND IN RESIDENTIAL USE, GREENSBORO, NORTH CAROLINA, 1960

physical or social environment, whether they are realized immediately, later or not at all.

Boguslaw proposes therefore to use the models as abstract social criticism, i.e. to use predictions and experiments in order to find policies which are not based on the extension of the present conditions. This approach, however, directly contradicts the present trend in our society, and the methods of the technocrats, namely, predictable policies which avoid conflicts, assure profits

and generate stable "system" developments. And who is ready to do this?

Example of a First Generation Model
The first generation models — understood as feedback instruments — are composed of complete sets or *interrelated* but not *interchangeable subsystems,* each of which has its own parameters, variables and constraints. Once the model is formed and balanced to an *equilibrium* it can hardly be changed and cannot correspond to changes in

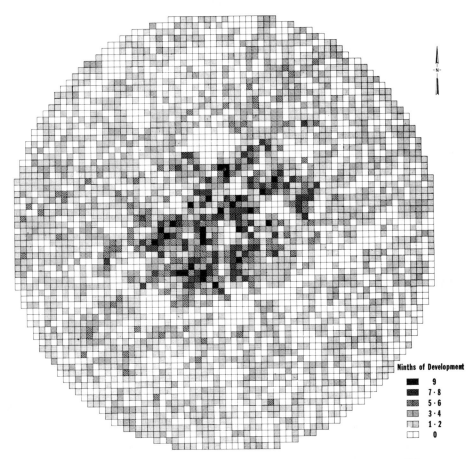

Ninths of Development

⬛	9
▨	7·8
▨	5·6
▨	3·4
▨	1·2
☐	0

**EXPECTED RESIDENTIAL LAND USE, GREENSBORO, NORTH CAROLINA, 1960
BASED ON USE OF PROBABILISTIC MODEL – MEDIAN OUTCOME OF 50 RUNS**

reality. Uncontrollable deviations require the construction of a new model.

The most representative one is Ira S. Lowry's model,[17] which is based on the Economic Study of the Pittsburgh Region and on RAND's Urban Transportation Study. It is "a computer model of the *'spatial'* organization of *'human activities'* within a metropolitan area" describing ". . . changes in 'key variables' such as the pattern of 'basic' employment, the efficiency of the transportation system, or the growth of population." There are two main assumptions: first, that industry is an exogenous basic sector which influences the urban system but which cannot itself be influenced and, second, that transportation has predominant importance.

The Lowry Model is an equilibrium model without time dimension. It contains the unrealistic assumption that land use succession and migration can *a priori* be limited to an optimum level. The inputs are based on the basic sector (exogenous to the model), distribution of

71

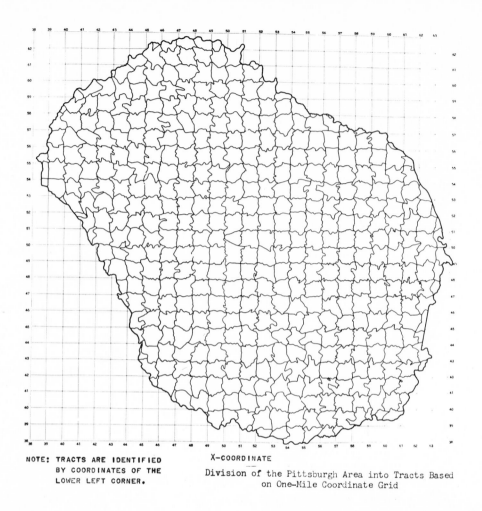

X-COORDINATE

Division of the Pittsburgh Area into Tracts Based
on One-Mile Coordinate Grid

retail and household sectors (endogenous) and the given size and value of the spaces they occupy. The output is a redistribution of locations derived from transportation data (distance, not time) and arranged by calculating interdependencies of the number and location of households vs. retail employment and location, both being dependent on the basic sector. The physical characteristics of land and legal restrictions upon it are further constraints. By combining these bits of information

with information about locations and accessibility, the model evaluates the potential of each location as a residential or retail site.

Distances are not concerned with time. The model's zones, areas or districts are determined arbitrarily by a square grid. Topological and sociological facts like naturally grown neighborhoods, rivers or hills can scarcely be integrated. Lowry's model is based on the "gravity" theory (the reciprocal relationship of distance and attraction).

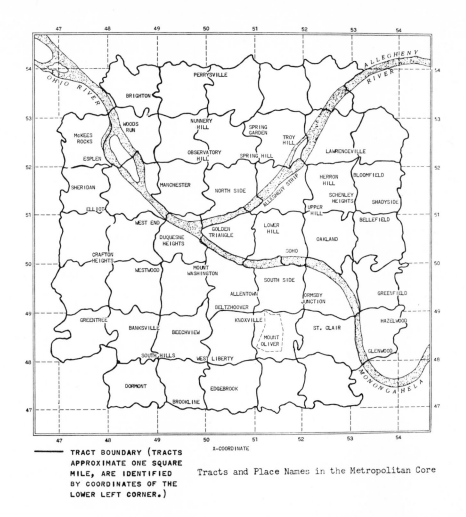

TRACT BOUNDARY (TRACTS
APPROXIMATE ONE SQUARE
MILE, ARE IDENTIFIED
BY COORDINATES OF THE
LOWER LEFT CORNER.)

Tracts and Place Names in the Metropolitan Core

This combines with the "generally accepted theory of the market for urban land" and with the fact that ". . . the most nearly comprehensive metric available in our society, whether we like it or not, is money."[18]

Even if this "generally accepted theory" of a perfectly competitive market were correct, it should not be applied within urban models. Lowry himself points out that the necessary data is unavailable and it is unrealistic to expect the continual publication of all market prices. But even if this information were available, the theory is not correct. Lowry naively reduces urban system behavior to — in the best case — simple location and migration, land use and land use succession. He says: "Urban spatial organization is the outcome of a process which allocates activities to sites. In our society, the process is mainly one of transaction between owners of real estate and those who wish to rent or purchase space for their homes and businesses. These transactions are contracts which are freely entered into, neither party having a legal obligation to accept the other's offer." [19]

Any plans based on this model will necessarily function according to "purchasing power" rather than to the needs of people for living space. When *"planning"* means *planning for the real estate market* it should not be called *"planning for urban activities."* In the best case, given the constraints of the basic sector's influence and even granting a purely competitive market behavior, Lowry's model can do nothing but design a more orderly, efficient and profit-making distribution of the given land under study.

Second Generation Models

The second generation models — understood as feedforward instruments — are composed of sets of *interchangeable subsystems* and are based on the assumptions that the modelled activities and their interdependencies should be comprehended within *a single framework;* that activities, physical growth, internal shifts and so on must be recorded within a *dynamic model* rather than an equilibrium model and that *timing* and *phasing* constraints must be integrated into the models.

Following these principles, Jay W. Forrester presents a feedback control-based *economic computer model,* "Urban Dynamics," [20] which describes the macroeconomic growth, stagnation and decay of cities over time. The model is derived from Forrester's "Industrial Dynamics," [21] a model designed for business processes which occur in relatively closed systems with rather clear goal orientation. From this limited scope he derives the assumption which becomes the hypothesis of "Urban Dynamics," that complex dynamic systems are: *"Counter-intuitive,* insensitive to system parameter changes, resistant to policy changes, possessing few *influential pressure points* that alter the sys-

tem balance, counteracting to externally applied corrective programs with counteracting short-term reactions and drifting to low performance." [22]

The model's background itself shows the general limitation. Business can only be one aspect of urban processes. So when the model deals with complex dynamic systems generally, it refers actually to purely economic problems generated more by the characteristics of capitalism than by those of complex systems.

Forrester employs the following technique to analyze the behavior of "dynamic (social) systems":

1. *Establishment of closed boundaries around the system.* In order to steer the system's behavior, system boundaries must be closed and purposes of the system performance must be known. This isolation provides the means to analyze qualitatively and quantitatively certain internal interactions, levels and rates, causes and effects. External factors are declared to be irrelevant.

2. Determination of the *relevant feedback structure* and the *basic structural elements* within the boundaries which determine the behavior of the systems. Feedback structures can be either negative or positive. Negative ones are goal-oriented; their interactions tend to maintain the system level and to prevent deviations. Positive feedback structures are growth-oriented.

The *feedback loop* consists of (a) the *level variables* representing accumulation and integration within the feedback loops and (b) the *rate variables* representing the amount of activity and quality of goals within the feedback loops. The rate variables, through their rate equations (statements of the system policy representing implicit goals and defining the system's behavior) regulate changes in the level while the level variables supply information back to the rate variables.

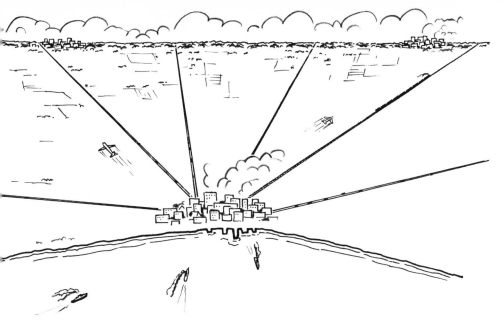

The urban area in its limitless environment.

Dynamic behavior
generated within the
boundary. Characteristic
modes of behavior created
by interactions within the boundary.

Closed boundary defining a dynamic system.

3. *Description of system level variables* which are calculated by the determination of discrepancies between the goals and observed conditions and of optioned actions and policies to correct these discrepancies.

The mystic cloud within the diagram represents sources or destinations from and to the outside environment, again exclusively controlled by the inside rate. As decisions are made exclusively by the rate equations implicit to each loop, no outside-effected change is considered to be possible. The model rates, however, may differ from true conditions since they come from model thinking and expectations rather than from real

situations. Accordingly, the rates, when transferred into policy, may change the system in unexpected ways.

The goal of "Urban Dynamics" is to model three urban activities — population, housing and industry (business). This justifies the restriction and omission of a variety of urban activities. Forrester argues irrationally, intuitively and purely economically:

The model is a selection, from numerous alternatives, of factors that are believed pertinent to questions about urban growth, ageing, and revival . . . the change in housing, population, and industry are the central processes involved in growth and stagnation. They are more fundamental than city government, social, cultural, or fiscal policy.[23]

To analyze the three activities and their interdependencies, Forrester first establishes artificial formal system boundaries according to his proposed analytical techniques and feedback control theory. While avoiding any discussion of the actual workings of his tech-

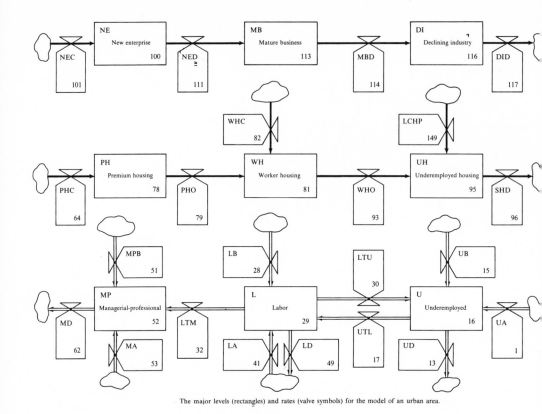

The major levels (rectangles) and rates (valve symbols) for the model of an urban area.

nique, he declares the city to be naturally a closed system with boundaries where two-sided interactions no longer occur; and he concludes that the country around the city, the suburbs and the national economy can be excluded from the model's integration, as they are one-sided influences. He argues:

The behavior of a city is much more directly dependent on its own economic merit and its changing internal mix of industry, housing and population . . . For our purposes the urban area can therefore be taken as a living system that communicates with an environment it does not substantially influence.[24]

The model then represents a *totally closed* system determined by the growth, maturity and stagnation of its three components: industry, housing and population. Those, broken into nine "subcomponents" synthesize the model to a self-regulating mechanism. Several model builders question Forrester's theory on the basis that he omitted consideration of external influences like the national economy, or the suburbs. It is necessary to go further, however, and question the assumption that a city can be a closed system at all. Forrester mentions the city of Berlin as an example which substantiates his theory. Therewith he contradicts himself, since this city on one side is really "closed," but on the other hand could never exist without its massive outside supports, with tax reduction, tax incentives to promote investment, constant campaigns to recruit new workers and large subsidies

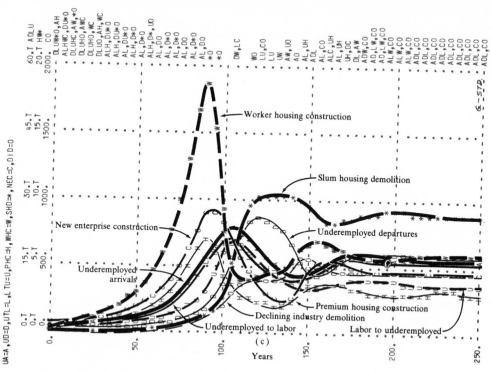

Urban development, maturity, and stagnation.

from the federal government to maintain city services and administration.

Forrester, analyzing the interdependencies of the three activities, further concludes that population and housing are interdependent sectors; industry, however, effects the change in the other sectors but is not substantially affected by them. Thus, industry is the driving force and its life cycle determines the whole system's behavior. This assumption seems to be realistic in some cases. But Forrester obviously accepts it uncritically, as implicitly within his model he considers the urban environment to be simply an abstract, limitless source which can supply and absorb people and resources just as industry needs them. That the city must meet needs generated by activities besides the selling of labor and the development of administrations remains irrelevant to him.

Forrester predicts and describes a 250-year life cycle for the present city, for any city, with the assumption that a normal balance between various activities exists before the process of city growth begins. During the first stage (100 years) the area grows into a city with increasing industry; between 100 and 200 years there is a period of maturation and internal readjustment, accompanied by the symptoms of stagnation and a declining tendency beginning at the age of about 140 years; and after 200 years there is a continuing equilibrium which includes all the negative symptoms of the city: the slums, the centers, the suburbs and so on.

77

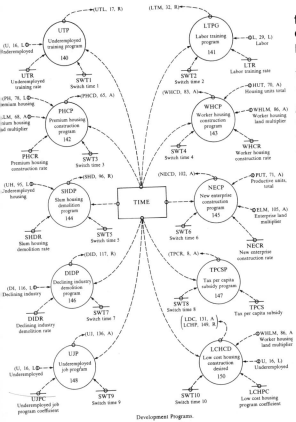

Labels in diagram:

(UTL, 17, R)

(U, 16, L○○—) Underemployed

UTP
Underemployed training program
140

UTR
Underemployed training rate

SWT1
Switch time 1

(PH, 78, L○—) Premium housing

—(PHCD, 65, A)

(LM, 68, A○—) nium housing ad multiplier

PHCP
Premium housing construction program
142

PHCR
Premium housing construction rate

SWT3
Switch time 3

(UH, 95, L○—) Underemployed housing

—(SHD, 96, R)

SHDP
Slum housing demolition program
144

SHDR
Slum housing demolition rate

SWT5
Switch time 5

(DID, 117, R)

(DI, 116, L○—) Declining industry

DIDP
Declining industry demolition program
146

DIDR
Declining industry demolition rate

SWT7
Switch time 7

(UJ, 136, A)

(U, 16, L○—) Underemployed

UJP
Underemployed job program
148

UJPC
Underemployed job program coefficient

SWT9
Switch time 9

TIME

(LTM, 32, R)

LTPG
Labor training program
141

○L, 29, L) Labor

LTR
Labor training rate

SWT2
Switch time 2

(WHCD, 83, A)

○HUT, 70, A) Housing units total

WHCP
Worker housing construction program
143

○WHLM, 86, A) Worker housing land multiplier

WHCR
Worker housing construction rate

SWT4
Switch time 4

(NECD, 102, A)

○PUT, 71, A) Productive units, total

NECP
New enterprise construction program
145

○ELM, 105, A) Enterprise land multiplier

NECR
New enterprise construction rate

SWT6
Switch time 6

(TPCR, 8, A)

TPCSP
Tax per capita subsidy program
147

TPCS
Tax per capita subsidy

SWT8
Switch time 8

LDC, 131, A
LCHP, 149, R

○WHLM, 86, A Worker housing land multiplier

LCHCD
Low cost housing construction desired
150

○U, 16, L) Underemployed

LCHPC
Low cost housing program coefficient

SWT10
Switch time 10

Development Programs.

One of the model's main purposes is to show how and when to *interrupt and intervene in* the life cycle with appropriate policies in order to prevent stagnation and to attain a prosperous equilibrium by finding "the few influential pressure points that alter the system's balance." Within this framework Forrester computes and exposes the ineffectiveness of the existing city renewal and low cost housing programs. He criticizes them for not considering the interdependencies of available jobs, job training programs, housing shortages, migration and so on. He sees clearly that, isolated and of short-range value, they worsen the situation. The criticism is true, but it does not require such an extensive model mechanism. The need

for interrelated programs was seen several years ago without the aid of a computer-based model.

Next, Forrester computes his proposal for improvement:

This chapter, after exploring several policies, concludes that urban revival requires demolition of slum housing and replacement with new business enterprise. Only by this shift from slum housing to new business will the internal mix become healthy.[25]

He predicts that by demolishing five per cent of a city's slum housing per year, one could achieve a fifty per cent rise in enterprises within fifty years, a fall of eleven per cent in underemployment, attractive housing (middle-income), no further migration and after fifty years, a continuous prosperity. So he believes that he has created a mechanism that is effective as a socio-economic converter to upgrade the poor to middle-class. Having achieved this "filtering and shifting process" Forrester proposes the creation of an artificial housing shortage (compare the strategies of oppression in World Dynamics) in order to maintain and control a dynamic equilibrium. "The resulting housing shortage restrains the population inflow which would otherwise defeat revival of the area."[26]

These consequences, however, abstractly computed, hide the actual processes. The generation of an industrial or business area will cause a shift from low-income to middle-income population through the attraction of middle-class residents and through the eviction and isolation of the "poor ones" who live in the modelled area. Forced to leave, they clear the area automatically and mechanically of the actual problems and carry them to the next or another area, having again no decent housing, no jobs and no health care. It is ultimately the model, based on "irrational" *economic* counter-intuition, that intervenes into their lives and expels them. And it is the model that prevents a solution based on human, rational "counter-intuition."

Forrester's conclusions show the actual power and danger of this model and its technocratic politics. Inhuman interventions deriving from "antisocial theories" (Forrester's expression) are justified with economic "counter-intuition" — purposive rationality for the sake of organized profit-making, balanced exploitation of the urban areas and the maintenance of social order and classes. The model itself, well removed from the greater social context and therefore irrational as a whole, becomes a dangerous instrument. It increases the power of scientific, inhuman organization, to implement scientific violence. Even more, it molds the environment into a purely economic business machine to which people must submit while ignoring all the inhuman consequences and by-consequences of this model, an instrument of technocratic fascism.

Forrester's faith in counter-intuition, economic rationality (pure purposive rationality) and the power of computers rigorously subordinates urban processes to business interests. Accordingly, his model fails in making the urban systems as social systems understandable, more human and bearable. The exclusion of the social dimension, excluded not only by the techniques employed but also by the possibilities admitted for interpretations, prohibits essential questions, such as, "why do we have these questionable economic, political urban structures?" and "what are the qualitative criteria for change?" As a whole, this type of model is an excellent example of technocratic purposive-rationality and simultaneously of capitalist irrationality.

The constantly repeated request by politicians and planners for more power to achieve better control of the urban condition becomes much clearer now. The power they desire will be directed more toward the control of urban profits, their continuity and predictability and the adaptive manipulation of the *status quo* than toward control of conditions which generate threatening effects on people within the urban environments.

Third Generation Conflict

The third generation models — understood as combined feedback and feedforward instruments — do not yet exist. They are conceived of as sets of *intersystems* for social communication, decision making and systems synthesis based on a core system generating and integrating new and different subsystems. This creation is a technocratic goal of interdisciplinary teams of model builders composed of experts from political science, sociology, behavioral science, economics, architecture, planning, operational research and cybernetics. The model builders point out that, if they are successful in designing the third generation models, the time will have come for the reintegration of the once eliminated human-related variables. But if this will simply mean the aggregation of positivistic, "value-free," black box, system-stabilizing adaptive methods, how can these third generation models differ qualitatively from the second? All indications are that they will again be "one-dimensional," understood and developed by the same narrow-gauged expertise. With this in view the hope for reintegration appears to be more ideological than real.

For approaching a more human and better urban environment, quantification models can only be helpful in addition to and in cooperation with qualitative analysis, and only if the model's *limitations,* now concealed behind the facade of pretended rationality and objective science, will be clearly realized and transcended:

— Limitations through the given model imperatives, the irrational predecisions, the simplified basic assumptions, the capitalist priorities and prefabricated interest goals, the model builders' and commissioners' motivations and their uncontrolled influence within the model building process and application.

— Limitations through the limited choice of urban activities and phenomena to be analyzed and their mechanical, mathematical and behavioral description based on economic, numerical and operational logic; through the incapability to produce general statements and satisfying explanations of causes and effects, and to deal with unavoidable consequences of unconsidered aspects of the model; through the uncontrolled manipulations of phenomena, in the best case representatively chosen, but later distorted and deleted.

— Limitations through the quantification of certain behavioral aspects of basic human functions and needs, assumed to be capable of evaluation and manipulation (such as calculations of people's consumer behavior); through the elimination of those needs which are considered non-exploitable (therefore often treated as unquantifiable and not additive); and through the neglect of deviant behavior and the marginal needs of the poor.

— Limitations through the transfer of existent models to other fields of application with the corresponding transfer of implicit sets of restrictions, assumptions and ideological priorities. This is evident in the transfer of transportation models and economic organization models, which deal with cars and profits, to the other urban activities which concern the lives of people.

Despite all these limitations, quantitative analysis nevertheless seems to be becoming the main goal of systems research. It has already created its own self-dynamic, attached to the capitalistic system and disassociated from people. It is ready to rush over the whole North American continent with the message of the new messiah. Enthusiastic responses come from all sides, for example when Kilbridge states:

We believe that analytical methods and especially symbolic methods will prove invaluable both in the development of the theory on which increasingly effective actions can be based, and as an aid to the decision-making which must proceed concurrently if our cities are to flourish.[27]

The technocratic victory of quantities, purposive rationalities and "push-button politics" over the quality of human life completes the triumph of the "how" over the "why."

VII. SOME SOCIAL CONSEQUENCES

Dreams of the Experts and New Utopian Engineers

Elite groups of experts and engineers who reduced transportation and industrial production complexities into quantitative predictable policies are now working on larger scales designing urban steering systems. To accelerate development and to integrate time-related planning, space researchers have been invited to join them. They promise us "a mechanism whereby those skills and assets acquired while working on the problems of defense and space can be transferred to problems of our cities."[1] The same experts who worked for years on the design of missile guidance systems, having succeeded in developing SIAM, PERT, MIRV, ABM and anti-guerrilla weapons will now work on "urban guidance and intervention systems."

However, the majority of technocrats will only shift their attention from rockets, jumbo jets and SSTs to large scale urban projects if industry and management shift their interests to the mass-production of cities.

On the other hand, as long as industries still meet their profit interests through the production of other technological products, as long as the present cities still work profitably enough with almost no investments in research or further development and as long as the pressure from the threatening population explosion is still too low to stimulate large scale profitable mass production of cities, we can assume that under the control of the capitalistic system the actual solution will be delayed.

Soon, however, the pressures of overpopulation on the cities will combine with falling profits in over-producing consumer industries to make further delays meaningless. At that point any solution to urban problems will seem legitimate and big business will have a free hand to undertake profitable mass production of cities. With this in mind, the industrial syndicates already are preparing — slowly, carefully and almost secretly — to safeguard their future profits. The International Telephone and Telegraph Company (ITT), for example, has already stated that it will be prepared to participate within the next decade in the "revolutionary" transformation of city production in the U.S. and abroad.[2]

The Ford Foundation has given large sums of money to universities like MIT to study urban systems. The computer companies, of course, have already begun to make huge profits from the research on systems and models following the directions already set by the Lowrys, Seidmans and Forresters who have set milestones and simultaneously outlined imperatives for their followers.

An architectural application of the modelling approach is Nicolaus Negroponte's "architectural machine"[3] based on "citizen feedback" which would establish the "human environment." Negroponte believes that he can circumvent the pragmatist's axiom that needs and desires are "not describable." He proposes using intelligent machines capable of learning, which

PROGRAM

◁*Following a year of experiments and exercises in 'artificial design intelligence', the Architecture Machine Group will start constructing a satellite machine which will be the beginnings of an Architecture Machine. This device will be primarily composed of Interdata processors and Interdata memory. Its task will be to learn about architecture.*

The following illustrations represent three particular experiments that have in common the specific goal of providing Architecture Machines with the ability to solicit information on their own.

The two diagrams are estimates of the first two years of growth.□

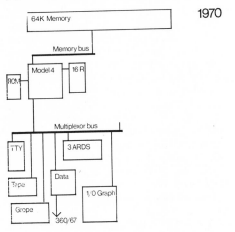

1970

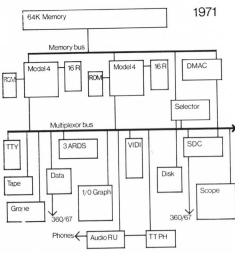

1971

can substitute for the circumstantial "black box" method and the application of behavioral science. Human beings then can have "natural" dialogues with the machine which "objectively" tests their behavior and intelligence and, according to Negroponte, adapts to the intelligence and behavior of the user. "The dialogue, in turn, must reside within a computer-aided (not computerized) system. The system, consequently, must include a "resident processor," some real world sensors and effectors and an intelligence."[4] Now the behavioral scientist can retire from analyzing his objects to devise instead conditioning strategies and practicable instruments.

Richard Hessdorfer has already tested "real world sensors" by establishing tele-devices operated by three individual inhabitants in Boston's South End. His euphoric surprise and his middle-class interpretation should be quoted here:

First, the three user-inhabitants said things to this machine they would probably not have said to a human, particularly to a white planner or politician: to them the machine was not black, was not white, and surely had no prejudice. Second, the residents had no qualms or suspicions about talking with a machine: they did not type uncalled-for remarks; instead they immediately entered into a discourse about slum landlords, highways, schools, and the like.[5]

Criticizing this experiment, we can say first that it shows very clearly the awareness and concern of the problem-affected people (which is stronger than the middle-class awareness), and second, that if those people had known that there was still a white planner, hidden consciously behind the pretense of a neutral machine, who was at MIT designing programs for and controlling the machine, and as likely as any planner to use the information gained against them, they would probably never have

"Natural" dialogues led by real world sensors

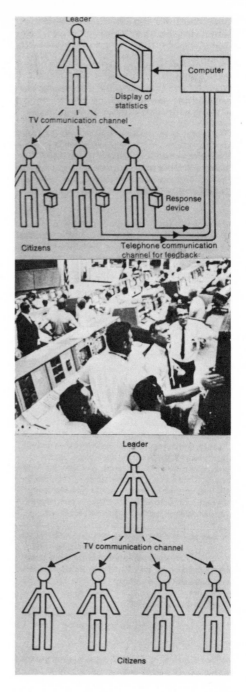

touched the tele-typewriter.

Chandler H. Stevens and Thomas B. Sheridan from MIT recently presented new, so-called "citizen feedback"[6] models. They developed computer-aided information systems based on the use of gadgetry from the communications revolution. Citizens participate as "competing" interest groups in political, social and planning decision processes, public hearings, group discussions and so on.

Both models, however, understand the participating citizens as isolated individuals. They therefore do not provide for the establishment of horizontal communications and face-to-face contacts necessary for building "competing interest groups." Accordingly, the leaders and decision-makers still have the power to manipulate the isolated participating individuals. Using preprogrammed models as instruments for faster and better manipulation, they can persuade people and anticipate unpleasant conflicts.

Extrapolating from these kinds of experiments we can imagine a large-scale urban planning machine, epitomizing the dream of the technocrats, for the production of new urban structures and as the control instrument for function, growth and change in both new and existing urban structures. If we imagine as well the establishment of as many environmental sensors as possible (from the utopias we learn about the idea that everyone must be connected to a sensor), then it is clear that this point where all urban and social data are collected and processed — Melvin Webber's *"urban intelligence center"* — becomes an enormous decision and power center for all kinds of interventions. Those who dominate the programs, machines, operations and policies have unlimited power over people. Considering the possibilities of the present technical and psychological means to prevent "horizontal communication," among people, one has to make every effort to keep the planning experts from extending their powers of decision and domination, especially when they talk in terms of human machines, human plans and "citizen feedback."

Boguslaw therefore proposes another alternative: the participation of the people whom the planning concerns, when the models and programs are first being built up. But this is not practical any longer because the building processes are already so specialized that only the experts and technocratic elites can handle them.[7] Even the scientists themselves become more and more alienated from the building processes which on

the whole they cannot understand.

Our argument has already raised, several times, the fact that publicly controlled institutions seem to be the only escape from the dilemma. Under this kind of control, concerned people could explicate and discover new needs, desires and value systems, not while isolated or confronted with an anonymous machine, but collectively with dialectic human argumentation. Since society consists of collectives, not of isolated individuals, collective qualitative decisions, not the isolated quantitative repetition of irrational, indoctrinating arguments, must be the parameters for planning models and social advancements. Decisions must evolve out of public institutions and not from technocratic centers. Controls must be exercised by the base of society in order to guarantee that the needs and desires of all people can be explored and freely mediated, without oppression or repression.

Unfortunately the pragmatic, conservative, libertarian and even the liberal planners and scientists who are involved in and daily experience these problems still believe that good and human solutions are possible within present capitalist structures. They refuse to understand that *effective democratic control* needs a new institutional legitimization to control the power elites, and new institutionalized mechanisms to make the people's demands effective in the realms of necessity and freedom. Waiting for miracles or operating exclusively in economic terms, they permit the ongoing urban massacres.

The Wholesaling of Urban Systems Analysis

Urban model builders and systems analysts constantly refer to the incompleteness and restricted capacities of their theories and models. Being scientifically oriented, they warn us away from practical application of their "scientific tools" on the technical grounds that the quality of the inner mechanisms is still imperfect and applicable only to small-scale problems.

The unsuccessful or incomplete results, however, stimulate the "scientific elite" to improve half-true schemata into "satisfactory results" and "qualified" tools. But instead of working on real qualitative improvements — which would require the introduction and translation of human-related and multi-dimensional value systems, variables and data — they devise higher technical specifications, more complete computer languages, better computer equipment and additional normative refinements. Controlled fundings, pressures of time and other irrational influences push them into expedient approaches. Discussion about the basic assumptions within the problem-question and problem-solution diminishes more and more in importance and relevance to the scientists' concerns.

The completed models are given to funding commissions and to experts and social engineers for transfer into practical tools and instruments. The last traces of the theoretical superstructure then are deleted. Original analyses are transformed into system techniques, beyond the control either of the scientists or of the public. The scientist as tool producer has done his job; he does not feel responsible for the social implications.

Second-hand applications of specified analyses may be the worst and most irresponsible results facing us in the future of the models systems approach. They become the "equivalent" devices used by "experts" who cannot afford the expenditures for project-oriented analyses and planning models. This results in inappropriate generalizations, wrong conclusions, transfer of nonexistent problems. Forrester's generalized *Urban Dynamics* invites exactly this kind of misuse, which in the end may constitute its most dangerous impact and failing.

Political Misuses

Liberal politicians, the technocrats and the social engineers have common goals: stability, continuity, neutralization and conflict avoidance through specific interventions. Although the power of the politicians is being restricted more and more by industrial management and technocrats, they understand their alliance with scientists and with the technocrats as a means of recovering their powers of manipulation and domination.

Scientists sell their half-true prototypes to the politicians who then simplify the results and use them as an aid in social manipulations, as we learn from Herman Kahn:

When one is preparing a briefing of fairly new ideas, especially when dealing with relatively unfriendly audiences, to have available the results of a large number of computations . . . it is very persuasive to answer objections by citing specific, detailed and relative numerical calculations.[8]

Politicians now attack and intervene openly, using impressive "rational" scientific arguments to convince people and communities to follow without resistance their plans and models. People should be impressed, manipulated and intimidated by the rational insights from the realm of necessity offered by the planner without realizing that the plan ultimately works against them.

This also is a substantial end of Forrester's urban analysis. It tries to explain technically that urban revival *mostly* depends on demolishing slums and preempting their territory for business and industries and the ostensible creation of new jobs. Of course, the people whose homes are torn down do not necessarily get those jobs, and so end up with neither jobs nor homes. Forrester's plan, however, works "scientifically," and therefore is strengthened by the great force of structural imperatives behind it. It removes the symptoms but not the illness.

Much more sophisticated "push-button" models are sold by the social scientists. For example, the Cambridge

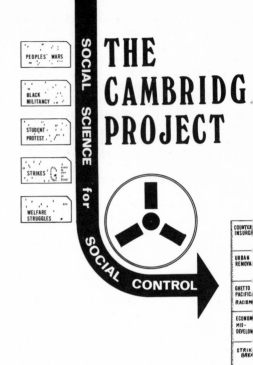

Project, funded by the defense department, solves such urban problems as how to "estimate the number of riots triggered by event Y because of communications pattern K given Q number of political agitators of type Z; or more generally, how to plan a coup in a country A where government B correctly assesses the needs of its people to be C and D and the trend in public opinion is becoming more and more favorable according to indicators F, G etc."[9]

Ithiel de Sola Pool, the framer of the Cambridge Project, talking about the "mandarins" of the future (the intelligentsia of the ruling class), once said that for "understanding the world around them . . . such knowledge is important to the mandarins of the future, for it is by knowledge that men of power are humanized and civilized."[10]

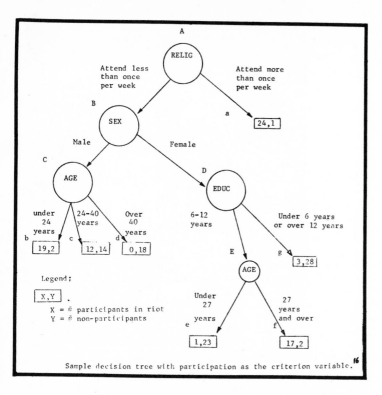

Sample decision tree with participation as the criterion variable.[16]

Legend:

| X,Y |

X = # participants in riot
Y = # non-participants

Common responses to ghetto rebellions, which have been designed in academic centers, have included: setting up youth patrols for community self-policing'; poverty programs in which youths are paid to go out and keep people cool and report on trouble-makers; and other projects whose purposes typically include buying-off potential leadership in ghetto uprisings. Thus while the history of ghetto revolts has shown their importance in generating lasting political organization and in enhancing political clarity among black people in their struggles against their oppression, the responses of the city bosses have been to try to prevent such developments at all costs.

But on the other hand he states that they also need "knowledge of the culture, values, social and political structures of every country that is a potential enemy, ally or scene of turmoil — and that is virtually all the world."[11] In other words, he urges the exercise of the newly developed scientific disciplinary instruments for social control and push-button politics — at home as instruments aganist strikes, welfare struggles, protests and unrest, mainly within the cities; and abroad, as instruments for imperialism, infiltration of ideologies, market expansions, oppression and warfare.

Knowledge, data accumulation, trend analysis, structure and functioning analysis, predictions, feedback and feedforward techniques are the actual modern means for social control and discipline. They are often projected into the future to be accompanied by the technological achievement of direct electronic control over individuals. Given these conditions, political power models gain more and more importance — already the first theoretical and probably practicable ones have been constructed, for example, by Karl Deutsch — in order to provide for the optimal and most efficient use of political power.

In all these advancements the universities play the most important part. They become the most effective means for producing and reproducing the present social conditions. The original concept of a neutral center for all kinds of education and research, which provides society with manpower and scientific means to solve its problems, remains a pure fiction. All important universities

89

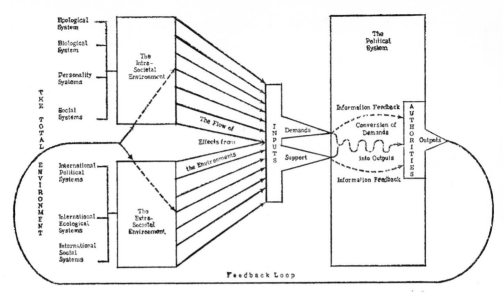

are in the hands of a small power elite which directs class and profit-oriented research and education. Representatives from military, political, industrial and financial sectors control them with funds and scholarships, and dominate them as trustees, corporation members, administrators and teachers. The university is successively perverted to a selective training center and a market place for elite research.

The pathological subordination of scientists, researchers, faculty members and of students, to time, performance and financial pressures closes the circle and makes the liberal choice of academic activities irrelevant; no matter which choice is taken, it is always dominated by the capitalistic forces.

Scientists and teachers must sell their products (research) and be concerned with appropriate commissions and fundings. This makes them vulnerable to every condition that promises to make profits. As professionals they fear losing their positions, social recognition and status. Therefore, when asked for political evaluations, they often keep silent and evade responsibility. The sci-

Models to provide for the optimal and most efficient use of political power and adaptation imperatives

entist isolates, separates, sets boundaries and dichotomies around himself and his research. He identifies with his self-constructed objectivity.

The Ideology of the "Liberated Subsystem"
In order to conceal the total dominating character of the capitalistic U.S., "System" concepts of "free subsystems" are used as a new ideology — like the ideology of free choice, considered to represent "the" alternative to Communism. Recent studies in organizational and systems research which focus on social systems and their relationships between "system and subsystem" seem to bring about renewed interpretations of democratic rights, individual freedom and citizen feedback.

From organization research we learn about the *self-responsible* and *self-determining* subsystem in horizontal functional social organizations. On the other hand, general systems theory

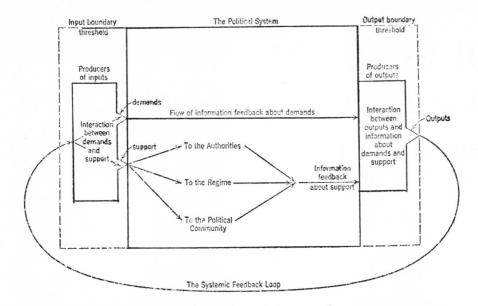

Input boundary | The Political System | Output boundary
threshold | | threshold

Producers of inputs | | Producers of outputs

demands

Flow of information feedback about demands

Interaction between demands and support

support

To the Authorities

To the Regime

To the Political Community

Information feedback about support

Interaction between outputs and information about demands and support

Outputs

The Systemic Feedback Loop

describes the whole system as an end, while it describes the subsystems as means. To a certain extent subsystems must be self-determining and self-regulating *per se* if the system is to be maintained and expanded.

The characteristics of a multistable system shows us that such a partial freedom and independence of the part-systems is necessary. Without this partial freedom of the part-system there is no higher development of the individual element and no higher development of the total system.[12]

Consequently, in considering individuals as subsystems of the society, the definition of "individual freedom" becomes a vital question less in terms of "free choices" but more in terms of the individual's impact on the system as a whole and his access to control.

Given the gap between our "individual systems" and the social system as a whole, it seems that the intelligent participation of all individuals is actually needed and that non-participation is basically excluded. Given the *horizontal* (as opposed to hierarchical) organiza-

tion of production and distribution systems, the potential for individual initiative seems greater than ever.

However, radical analysis exposes these arguments as purely formal ones. Much as they tried, analysts could not find qualitative differences in the behavior of people between hierarchical systems and the new kinds of organizations composed of "liberated subsystems" and the climate of a "free spirit." *Formal* system changes do not change the *substantial character* of the system. Hidden stop-rules, subtle controls, residual hierarchical influences, and regulations within the systems neutralize the formal freedom and maintain well-defined human role-behavior.

Extra-organizational factors, however, dominate the behavior of the individual subsystem even more. New methods of desire stimulation and behavior control manipulate the individual psyche in such a way that the results can be used most effectively for commercial and political purposes. Recent results in genetics, behaviorism and drugs for behavior modification make visions of total social control even more realizable.

Behavior pills for children used in Hub

By Herbert Black, Globe Staff

Drugs to impove the learning ability and school behavior of hyperactive children are being given in Boston and surrounding communities, but under strict medical supervision and not in large-scale programs.

Use of drugs to help correct behavior and learning problems of children who "can't sit still long enough to learn" became a controversial issue here this week. A Boston Globe-Washington Post dispatch on Monday reported 5 to 10 percent of the school children in Omaha, Neb., were being given drugs in behavior by their doctors. Radio talk shows here have been deluged with calls and in Washington two Federal investigations of the Omaha program were ordered.

Children who appear to be helped are those who are so active they can't sit still long enough to learn. They have such a short attention span they can't concentrate. They jump to conclusions instead of forging ahead to read the answers.

Other centers of study and treatment of hyperactive children with drugs include the Tufts-New England Medical Center, Children's Hospital Medical Center and Joseph P. Kennedy Jr. Memorial Hospital. Many individual pediatricians are prescribing the drugs.

Just how many children are being given drugs in this area cannot be estimated. Some physicians agreed that it was not out of line for 5 to 10 percent of an elementary school to have problems. Other doctors thought it was high.

A survey made last night indicates that many children are being helped by the drugs, that doctors agree children do not become addicted to the pills, that the drug program should never be undertaken indiscriminately and that each case should be judged individually and weighed carefully.

Dr. Leon Eisenberg, psychiatrist-in-chief at the Massachusetts General Hospital, a pioneer in the use of Dexadrine and Ritalin, said last night it would be tragic if overreaction hindered sound programs that used these drugs to help children who need help.

He said that the drugs "are safer than aspirin" for children. Most other doctors agreed with him that these stimulants, which can become physiologically addictive to adolescents and adults, are safe and none-addictive for children. Some doctors expressed reservations, however, about the long-term effect, asking whether it was a good thing to get children into a habit of taking pills?

Dr. Eisenberg and Dr. C. Keith Conners said they have treated 70 to 80 children a year since 1967 at the MGH Child Development Laboratory with no ill effects. They reported that two thirds of their treatments have been beneficial to the children.

But the doctors, who have done studies in private schools here and in public schools in Baltimore before coming to Boston, insist each child be given a battery of tests, that the medication be given by a nurse, that the parents understand and give permission and that it is determined the child's problems are not caused by either the teacher or other members of the immediate family.

They both agreed that the drug can be stopped at any time without any withdrawal symptoms. The effects of each pill lasts about six hours.

One of the problems of the drugs in large-scale application would be supervision to see they don't get into the wrong hands.

Drs. Eisenberg and Conners have found that, oddly enough, Dexadrine and Ritalin, which are 'pep' pills for older people, have the opposite effect on children. With them it acts as if it were a tranquilizer. This effect generally lasts until the age of 12.

The use of the drugs in helping overcome behavior and learning problems is now new, but doctors still don't know exactly how the drugs work. The work at the MGH is both clinical and research, but the doctors feel the clinical therapy has been proven.

Boston Globe, Wednesday, July 1, 1970   **3**

Where "passive adaptation" fails, interference with individuals becomes legalized

On the other hand, there are the internalized status orientations that generate the imperatives of mobility and docile behavior, resulting in alienated families and commercially exploitable anxieties. Marcuse refers to the acceptance of the present total domination as subordination under inhuman conditions for the sake of easiness. P. Baran and P. Sweezy say it most comprehensively: "The character of the system determines the psychology of its members and not vice versa." [13]

It is possible, however, that the concept of the "liberated subsystem" will become functionalized over all levels of society as a new principle of "system rationalization." Absorbed by several ideologies, it already substitutes for critical self-determination and participation. Integrated into the business world, it is repeated over and over to encourage individuals to adapt efficiently:

We will appreciate your willingness and your enthusiasm to obey rules and to avoid misunderstanding.

Be proud of your job because You will play a key role.[14]

Resisting Subsystems

Along with the subsystem "the individual," social groups or certain social processes can also be considered as social subsystems. They are less adaptive and sometimes show extremely strong self-dynamics: for example, the capitalistic society considered as a whole phenomenon; the dominating subsystem of purposive rationality; or certain political formations. Threatening influences from self-dynamic subsystems can be of two kinds: their functioning may create structural imperatives affecting the whole system; or, when unable

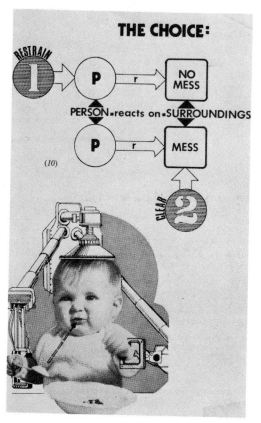

THE CHOICE:

PERSON reacts on SURROUNDINGS

(10)

to adapt, they become isolated and troublesome. Abolishing threatening subsystems however, means simultaneously removing their components — the "System" approach against critical political groups and organizations. Martin Oppenheimer describes the general process:

Each element in a system is also a kind of "subsystem," consisting in turn of other elements. Alterations in these elements, and in the links among them and between them and their subsystems or larger systems (super-systems or meta-systems), all cause structural strain. Other elements must "catch up" or change in turn so as to remove strain and enable the system to function once more in more normal terms. Since change is inevitable, structural strains are constantly present in social systems; and when there are deeply serious strains, or multiples of them, in a social system, it can no longer cope with its problems. In such circumstances the strains in the system affect many individuals so that they organize themselves to make the kinds of changes in the system they see as necessary to the creation of "a more satisfying culture." They seek a system in which strains have been alleviated sufficiently as far as the participants are concerned.[15]

Many subsystems can be dissolved by sufficiently strong and properly applied environmental power. This kind of dissolution has a special importance within the oppressive systems of total capitalistic or fascist societies. If specific subsystems do not adapt, they are threatened by environmental control, gradual or sudden, and violent or subtle dissolution. The slums to be removed become first economically, financially, or personally infiltrated and later structurally changed or demolished; oppositional political groups are supervised and persecuted by the FBI and local police and suffer from repeated imprisonment of their political leaders.

Attempted dissolutions and interventions fail, however, where situations are wrongly analyzed, strong subsystem-structures disregarded or where spontaneous and complex social systems spring up. The people in Vietnam, confronted with the U.S. "System's" naked power, developed enormously strong and self-defensive social subsystems; self-defensive, as they are concerned with their pure survival, and aggressive, as they, in turn, are forced to undermine, to isolate and to remove the threatening system's conditioning subsystems. The students in America react with alternative life styles, new non-prosperity-oriented value systems, the escape into underground life, physical demolition, psychological threats and sometimes threats of violence.

When we again consider all the ideologies, misuses and tendencies within systems research, model building processes and computer technologies, and when we relate them to the present tendency toward a technocratic society under the capitalistic system, we face a serious move toward a totally oppressive mechanical society. We face a society and world established by the technocratic engineers, dominated and alienated by all kinds of one-dimensional physical and electronic systems which arbitrarily change their properties from once liberating to now oppressing. A world which is now going to be formed, oppressed, manipulated and changed by the new utopian social engineers. Then the idea of critical non-alienated democratic *participation* in social processes will finally be *technocratically* eliminated. It may be that, for ideological reasons ruins of the concept remain within flexibly designed systems, where *formal* participation is open as far as possible, but *effective functional* participation is excluded.

a SLAVE is one who waits for someone to free him.

VIII. ALTERNATIVES

Alternatives: Radical and Revolutionary Planning

In the United States the development toward the total mechanical capitalistic model of a society meets increasing resistance — not primarily from the body of the middle classes, the silent majority which has learned to repress high grade alienation in the realm of necessity and freedom — but from those people who are most alienated and affected by poverty, unemployment, racism, environmental decay, urban massacres and class conflicts; i.e., those who are aware of and who experience daily the promised "prosperity," "affluent society" and the "free world," as pure ideologies. Militancy, riots, ghetto rebellions, bombings, hijackings, unrest, protests, radicalization and the youth counter-culture are the sporadic and spontaneous expression of the growing but still unorganized resistance. What happens in the U.S. is just the tip of the iceberg.

Abroad, third world countries and U.S. satellites are developing full-blown revolutionary situations. While reactionaries try to repress the signs of resistance with all available means, the liberals preach gentle integration of the challenges, and the technocrats simply ignore the social problems presented to them; even so, the resistance grows still stronger.

Most planners, liberal and conservative, feel that they are not attacked and

A desperate answer of the ghetto and slum-dwellers — Open armed class-struggle, urban guerilla warfare and bombing

within their work are far removed from these challenges. Their middle or upper class positions and their one-dimensional professional training provide psychological protection against attacks coming from the upset base of society. Only a few — the left-oriented critical radical planners — feel concerned about and respect the general challenges against the present social conditions and relate them to themselves and to their profession. They begin to understand and to analyze their class-bound function in society. They study more seriously the impact of their purposive-rational methods and products, and they understand that they must quit the field of mere technocratic planning in order to approach the multi-dimensional task of planning for a whole society. This task cannot be accomplished simply by the introduction and integration of new scientific rationalizing normative and empirical methods and theories, like the system approach to planning, the interdisciplinary or operational approach.

Radical planners analyze and question the existence of planning subject and planning object, their roles, function in society and relations to each other. Radical planners gradually begin to question their concepts of planning, their methods, the image of the profession, their professional and practical training, their own value systems and those of their clients. They see that purely "rational" planning methods, removed from a broader social context, do violence to people. In view of this, they abandon their former "natural" acceptance of given structural imperatives. Some of them even leave the planning field temporarily in order to gain the necessary perspective for reorientation. Their goals are clear: finding new methods to overcome the rigid division into planning commissioner, planner and user, into theory and practice, into perceiving and acting. They seek a new understanding of society, of human relations, of human needs and their satisfaction, of democratic principles and of the city itself, which is to be again a place of *emancipation* and *liberation* from oppressive conditions — within the realm of necessity *and* the realm of freedom. Publicly controlled institutions must become centers for autonomous citizen decision-making, rather than for irrelevant training in democratic behavior. In the place of "capitalistic prosperity," human and liberating principles must become the priority and must be *institutionally affirmed.*

The radical planners understand the planner's role as *subjective* (which was actually always the case). They understand themselves as either representative of the planning commissioners or of the people who are considered as the "planning objects." They take part actively in public decision-making processes and explicate their positions in social contexts. The *objective optimal* technocratic solution is excluded *per se.* It is replaced by the *subjective optimal* solution according to the objective needs of the user.

These needs cannot be discovered or rendered explicit, however, with isolated, randomly selected interrogations, surveys and statistics, nor with computer sensors and citizen feedback systems which accept and reproduce every kind of irrationality. Both ways are reproductive and non-creative. They lead either to distorted or banal results; results which simply reflect the needs which are manipulated by the capitalis-

53. And how much do you think your (city/town) officials are concerned about what people like you think--<u>very concerned, fairly concerned,</u> or <u>not too concerned</u>?

☐ VERY CONCERNED

☐ FAIRLY CONCERNED

☐ NOT TOO CONCERNED

176. To improve the conditions of life in this city, some say that people must get together to help themselves. Others say that the government must solve the problems. Do you think people should rely on themselves or the government?

☐ HELP THEMSELVES

☐ GOVERNMENT MUST SOLVE PROBLEMS

☐ BOTH

180. People differ in how much they like to plan things out. Would you say you <u>plan everything</u>, <u>plan a lot of things</u>, <u>plan a few things</u>, or <u>plan almost nothing</u>?

☐ PLAN EVERYTHING

☐ PLAN A LOT OF THINGS

☐ PLAN A FEW THINGS

☐ PLAN ALMOST NOTHING

Selling and purchasing individuals with simplified, rhetorical surveys

tic system. Potential human needs, including the need to experiment, remain repressed and do not appear[1] for the majority of the people. How can we expect to discover new and liberating needs without interrupting the rigid and closed circle of manipulation and reproduction? This will require alternative and new methods of investigation, as Claus Offe indicates:

It is a characteristic of social needs and interests, that they cannot be articulated by asking isolated individuals who are exposed to collective communication and direct confrontation with the situation which is under discussion. The normal case is that the isolated interviewee can only articulate his needs roughly and vaguely. Only in a concrete discussion do I have the opportunity to become aware of my own interests.[2]

In this sense Rittel's conflict-generating and decision making machine[3] seems to be effective. On the one hand it shows a positive tendency: namely, discuss your problem first, in

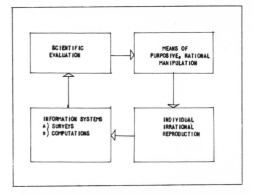

order to make your needs and desires clear to yourself; but then decide. On the other hand it shows a very negative tendency: namely, a pluralistic and numerical concept of decision processes which, lacking evaluative capacity, easily eliminates the quality gained in argumentation.

Several liberal planners and architects propose open alternative environmental *avant garde* solutions to suit the society that they envision for the future. They expect that once they create *"open doors,"* society will pass through those doors, thereby being converted. Change, however, will never come through visual or functional open environments. People will still be dominated by the system's social patterns. Neither the new environments nor the new scientific methods are the "problem worrier"[4] and the "problem solver." These are the people and planners with human rational political consciousness who are willing to solve the social problems by exploring real needs and by breaking through the given implications with all available means.

They face imperatives which create groups dichotomously participating and nonparticipating with or without intentions, goals, profits, capital, knowledge or apathy. Therefore, some planners research potential activities and communication channels between all planning participants and the people concerned. They locate the actual power positions in order to restrict them and to involve the concerned people most effectively. An ideal *planning collective,*[5] however (i.e., equal personal participation for everyone), cannot be realized in our present structure of a

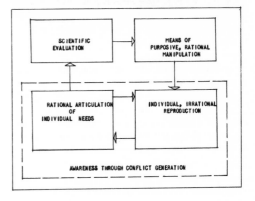

Middle and bottom: Awareness of needs through conflict generation and concrete discussions

capitalistic industrial society, for the planning group, composed of members whose skills, power and influence are too different, would be incapable of making equitable and workable decisions. The power of the participating experts, however, becomes relativized when they are forced to explicate and discuss their planning intentions and objectives to the whole "planning system." Once the people concerned are able to understand the intentions and assumptions of the planning experts, they are able to object and create substantial conflicts which strengthen their power of control within the planning process and their choice of the methods to be applied. Only this kind of planning process can generate new solutions; solutions which grow out of self-determination and self-education in non-alienated users. And only if these planning processes are institutionalized will the people achieve widespread social and political influence on the environment.

A distorted version of these ideas, combined with the concept of pluralism, is the recently popular "advocacy planning"[6] which is now being initiated in a few cities. It is an intermediate solution, since the division between planning subject (the scientific and expertocratic planning authority or organization) and planning object (the people concerned, their desires, needs and goals) is rigidly retained. The planner-advocate, a mediator between the people concerned, the methods and the commissioner, acts as "lawyer" and champion for solutions which favor the people. However, for poorer people as clients, this almost never works. Isolated from the planning clique by his commission and from his clients by his middle class position, the planner-advocate can neither fully understand his clients' needs and value systems nor wield sufficient power within the planning organization. Furthermore, the people concerned are completely dependent on the actions of the advocate who can render their desires non-effective and consciously or unconsciously exclude specific groups from participation.

Political and educational power, given into one person's hands, remains dangerous, especially when the planner-advocate, whose function is to provide for participation must at the same time accept capitalism as given and good. Caught within this contradiction, communities and users gradually lose interest in advocacy schemes.

Participatory Planning vs. the Systems Approach

The concept of *citizen participation* was introduced in the U.S. by the liberals after World War II with the hope of revitalizing *democratic participation* for the *socially alienated* and *disintegrated people* while maintaining the basic capitalistic structures. Since participation contradicts both the general concepts of *voted representation* and of capitalistic *free private* investment-decision, there is small hope for its realization. Due to the consequent compromises, participatory planning is weakened, restricted and ideologically misused by capitalistic and bureaucratic agents. "Participatory planning" as it is practiced today has failed because: although an instrument of public control . . . it has no institutionalized decision or veto power; instead of being an instrument for revealing unknown needs . . . it is used as an instrument for the extension of middle class needs; instead of functioning as a conflict-solution instrument . . . it is used as a conflict-avoiding instrument.

Several liberal models and strategies for participation have been developed, such as "education therapy," "behavioral change," "staff supplement," and "community power."[7] These strategies, however, depend strongly upon the participating planner professionals. If the planners and the concerned people stem from the same class — which is mostly the case within the affluent suburbs — participation "works well." The planner can easily represent and mediate by himself the interests, needs and value systems of his own class. In this situation, participation is hardly needed. It becomes a facile democratic game.

If the planner and the concerned people stem from different classes — which is mostly the case within poor inner city communities — participation is *misused* or *fails* completely. So the middle class planner, dependent on his specific *system of perception* and *mental categories,* ignorantly conceives of "poor people" as "strange, puzzling creatures"[8] who are very, very backward. Sometimes, he rationally accepts the poor as people, but seldom emotionally; so his capacity for communication and interaction with this class and its value systems is either superficial or completely blocked.

Working within the conservative ethic "that emotions of whatever kind should be less compelling forces than appeals to the rational self-interest,"[9] the middle-class professionals have eliminated emotional elements from their value systems. Self-denial, hard work and the postponement of "pleasures and amusement" are rewarded with economic advantages. These advantages form the basis for family, friends and community attachments and for the status-oriented conspicuous consumption. The poorer people are understood as consisting of individuals who are "improvident, irresponsible, without strong attachment to family, friends, or community and unable or unwilling either to control impulses or to put forth any effort at self-improvement."[10]

Poverty and repression are considered to be a given; so Banfield gives lower class people the fatherly advice to escape individually from their destiny and degradation. Banfield's argumentation shows the middle class helplessness and incapability of understanding the basic social values of the lower classes, as Richard Sennett says:

It has evidently not occurred to Banfield that the ghetto is a web for all sorts of decent people — not just the militants — whose sense of fraternity and concern for other people lead them to stay rather than to "put forth an effort at self-improvement by deserting family, friends and communities."[11]

Next page: Example of participation model

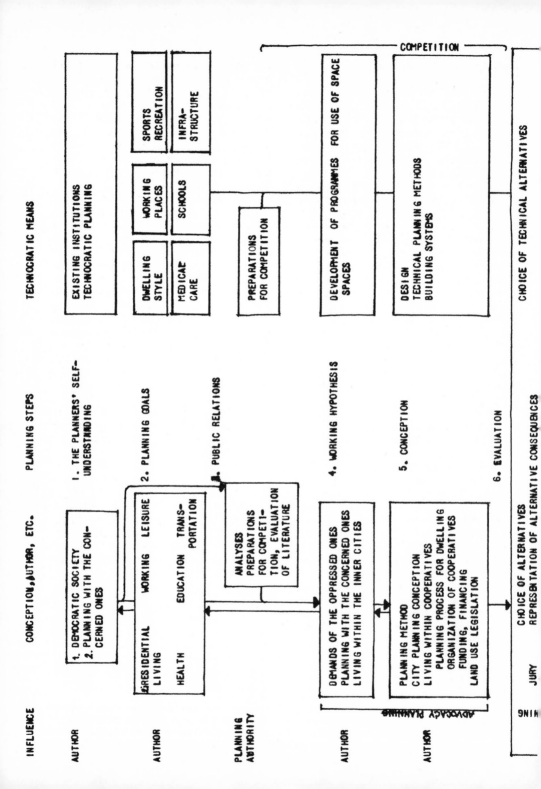

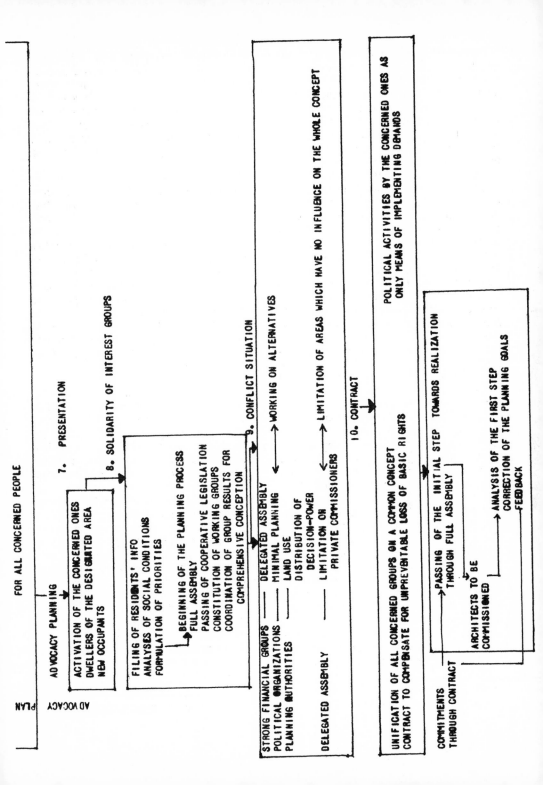

Banfield ignores the fact that *"self-improvement"* is part of the conservative middle class ideology and is mostly irrelevant to the lower classes. Isolated individuals liberated from the lower classes become entangled in even worse situations. They can liberate themselves only as a whole class, and they are on their way to doing just that.

People know that "participation" should mean much more. It should be self-determined, generating education, consciousness and awareness of needs and values, effective and functional project participation, development of equalized and workable decision control — all on economic, political and administrative levels. This would lead finally to control by the people of property conditions, institutions, means of production and to a stepwise abolishment of the social classes.

People also know that effective participation and worthwhile involvement can happen only within guaranteed coherent long-range and well-coordinated community programs (housing, medical, job, educational resources), which the participants and people concerned can easily control by themselves, economically, politically and administratively so that the experts play a secondary role. This would mean decentralized aid absorption, project- and area-oriented, handled without intervention by national or local authorities, or without the interference of middle class demands, supervision or profit-taking. Then the poor communities themselves, and not only the affluent suburbs, could autonomously control and manage the projects, programs and money.

With these objectives participatory planning strongly contradicts the capitalistic system in general, but also more specifically the scientific urban large-scale systems and model approaches. The prefabricated *centralized* planning approaches designed by middle and upper class scientists will soon conflict violently with *decentralized* participation and render it functionally ineffective. Then participation, if considered at all within the systems approach, will become an irrelevant, distorted and simplified yes-or-no participation, a combination of mute applause and silent discontent.

Those planners who engage in the present practice of *participatory planning* should consider why it is that, despite all their good will and individual efforts, their actions always end with misinformation about the people's needs, with adaptation imperatives, repressions, the destruction of emotional and group coherences, and the organized assassinations of communities. And what is their strategy to oppose the ever-farther-reaching large-scale technocratic system and model planning instruments which make participation less and less effective?

Revolutionary Planning
The revolutionary planning concept is based on a theory of cognition which overcomes the positivistic division between theory and practice, method and content, cognition and action, subjects and objects, science and politics, labor and capital, the realm of necessity and the realm of freedom. This change is based on the following considerations: cognition is inherent in action and is therefore always directed to practical applications which, in turn, require socially integrated human-related pre-scientific considerations. These inhibit the uncontrolled, one-sided dynamic of cognition and irrational application of purely "objective," "efficient" and "optimized" methods. Thereby pretended *scientific objectivity* can be exposed, questioned and turned into *social objectivity,* where the bound-

Response to the middle class planners' ideas of urban renewal

WEST END PROJECT
UR MASS. 2-3
A PROJECT OF
BOSTON REDEVELOPMENT AUTHORITY
AND THE
CITY OF BOSTON
THIS LAND ASSEMBLY AND REDEVELOPMENT PROJECT IS
BEING UNDERTAKEN WITH FEDERAL AID
UNDER TITLE 1 OF THE HOUSING ACT OF 1949
THROUGH THE
URBAN RENEWAL ADMINISTRATION
HOUSING AND HOME FINANCE AGENCY

TO HELL WITH URBAN RENEWAL!
IT IS LEGALIZED THEFT OF PRIVATE PROPERTY
WE SHALL DEFEND OUR HOMES WITH OUR LIVES

- THE BOSTON REDEVELOPMENT AUTHORITY WITH THE SUPPORT OF MAYOR COLLINS AND MEMBERS OF THE CITY COUNCIL, DESIRES THE TAKING AND DEMOLITION OF THESE HOMES SO THAT A PRIVATE REAL ESTATE SPECULATOR MIGHT BUILD ON THIS LAND HIGH-RENTAL, LUXURY APARTMENTS FOR PRIVATE PROFIT.
- IS THIS NOT DISCRIMINATION IN HOUSING?
- THEIR LYING PROPAGANDA CALLS THIS NEIGHBORHOOD "BLIGHTED"/ WHAT DO YOU THINK?
- THE ONLY BLIGHTED PROPERTY BELONGS TO A NEARBY UNIVERSITY.
- FORCED ENTRY TO OUR HOMES HAS BEEN MADE UNDER THREAT OF OFFICIAL REPRISAL.
- OUR WOMEN HAVE BEEN SHAMED AND HUMILIATED AND OUR PEOPLE PUT IN FEAR.
- LIKE HEARTLESS COWARDS, ALL OUR CIVIC AND RELIGIOUS LEADERS HAVE DESERTED US.
- THE PRESS HAS BETRAYED US AND THE PUBLIC AT LARGE REMAINS UNINFORMED OF OUR PLIGHT.
- *BUT AS FREE AMERICANS WITH GOD GIVEN RIGHTS THAT GUARANTEE THE SANCTITY OF OUR HOMES, WE SHALL PREVAIL AGAINST THE LAND THIEVES, NO MATTER WHAT THE COST.*

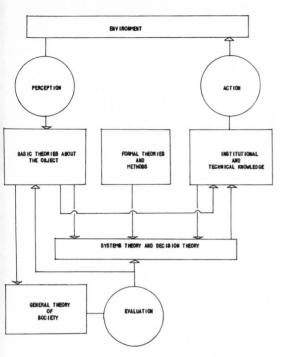

Coordination of a body of environmental knowledge

aries between science and politics and the dependence of labor on capital no longer exist. This requires the simultaneous integration of all traditional social and formal sciences. For that task the application of cybernetic sciences can be very useful. The practical sciences are used to predict the outcome of planned environmental, social and economic change. Ultimately, revolutionary planning requires the general theory and model of a classless, socialistic free society with its human-rational defined goals which let the realm of freedom appear within the realm of necessity and which abolish all the antagonistic contradictions in society. The general theory operates as measures to all economic, social, political and cultural actions.

All such planning, then, is based

upon the recognition of the biological and psychological facts of the human life cycle and on its natural and social relationships.[12] The *human dynamic process model of society,* based on ongoing discussions and the needs of the working people, eliminates antagonistic contradictions and integrates continual dialectic classificatory corrections, varying degrees and intensities of free associations and disassociations, interactive processes and activities that at all levels and stages reflect the socialistic development of society and its theory. Small-scale decentralized planning, then, is understood as anticipating, predicting and steering productive and reproductive processes based on the *critical social and constructive technical sciences* and according to fundamental social and technological changes and developments. *Effective participation* becomes a central social function. The institutionalization of all kinds of *participatory autonomous planning systems* on economic, political and administrative levels prevents any division between planning-subjects and planning-objects, planning-producers and planning-consumers. Planning goals and objectives are collectively determined and articulated according to the desires and needs of a participating

Organization of comprehensive planning

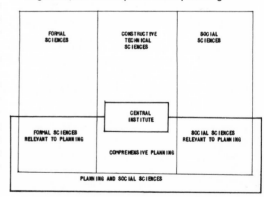

106

and concerned people and according to general social theory and developments. Participating experts have to explicate and allow critiques of their planning methods, models and substance. Normative and purposive-rational methods like the urban systems and planning models are critically developed and consciously applied. They must be related to and evaluated with non-purposive-rational value systems. Optimization and economic rationality become no longer the matter of maximized profits but of *maximized satisfaction of human needs* with minimized social expenditures. This necessitates the construction of those urban models which provoke or integrate easily human-oriented advancements.

Large-scale centralized planning, understood to act as an *integrating* and *coordinating system* over all various small-scale projects and planning fields needs to be established to avoid entanglements, overlappings, isolations and contradictions. This planning has an informative and recommending function and no executive power. Regional planning is needed to mediate between the central coordinating system and the small-scale decentralized planning projects. All three levels must be combined through public discussions dealing with their conflicts and solutions.[13]

This kind of planning, applicable to social, economic, political, physical, educational and research planning problems, becomes less irrational. It serves, for all participants, as a socio-political *learning* and *experimental* instrument providing them with *human-rational* insights into the society as a whole. It eliminates the irrationalities in its ends and allows for human-rational production and social reproduction on all levels of society.

Revolutionary ideas, however, have little chance of being implemented within the present framework of the capital-

Planning model for a non-oppressive society

istic system. There are too many counter-revolutionary agents: the manipulators, the bureaucracies, the experts, the imperatives, the methods, the ideologies, the trends, the politics, the irrationalities and the dependency of labor on private and monopoly capital. The revolutionary American planners concerned about basic change in this society are aware that ideas for human-rational planning, in themselves, have almost no impact on social conditions (consider the overwhelming critique on the Vietnam War which couldn't stop it). They therefore orient themselves toward social developments which build "objective conditions" for revolution-

Next page: The people's model of a police department for Berkeley, California

"COMMUNITY—CONTROL—OF—POLICE"

DOCK OF THE BAY
Dock of the Bay 10/28/69

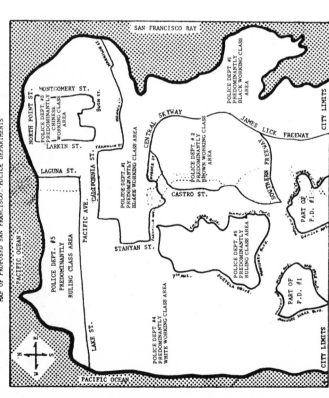

MAP OF PROPOSED SAN FRANCISCO POLICE DEPARTMENTS

SAN FRANCISCO BAY

PACIFIC OCEAN

PACIFIC OCEAN

CITY LIMITS

CITY LIMITS

POLICE DEPT #1
PREDOMINANTLY BLACK WORKING CLASS AREA

POLICE DEPT. #2
PREDOMINANTLY BROWN WORKING CLASS AREA

POLICE DEPT. #3
PREDOMINANTLY CHINESE WORKING CLASS AREA

POLICE DEPT. #4
PREDOMINANTLY BLACK WORKING CLASS AREA

POLICE DEPT #4
PREDOMINANTLY WHITE WORKING CLASS AREA

POLICE DEPT. #5
PREDOMINANTLY RULING CLASS AREA

POLICE DEPT #5
PREDOMINANTLY RULING CLASS AREA

PART OF P.D. #1

PART OF P.D. #1

MONTGOMERY ST.
NORTH POINT ST.
LARKIN ST.
BUSH ST.
LAGUNA ST.
FRANKLIN ST.
CALIFORNIA ST.
PACIFIC AVE.
LAKE ST.
STANYAN ST.
CASTRO ST.
CENTRAL SKYWAY
JAMES LICK FREEWAY
SOUTHERN FREEWAY
7TH AVE.
PORTOLA DRIVE.

PEOPLE'S POLICE DEPARTMENT

DIAGRAMMED FOR ONE OF OUR CITY'S POLICE DEPARTMENTS

EXAMPLE: A PEOPLE'S POLICE DEPT, WITH 7 NEIGHBORHOOD DIVISIONS,

THE PEOPLE OF THE PRECINCTS:
IS PRECINCTS PER NEIGHBORHOOD DIVISION,
THE PEOPLE IN EACH PRECINCT ELECT A POLICE COUNCILMAN,
QUALIFICATIONS FOR POLICE COUNCILMEN ARE

ELECTED

POLICE COUNCILS FOR THE **NEIGHBORHOOD DIVISION:**
THE 7 NEIGHBORHOOD DIVISIONS EACH HAVE A 15 MAN
POLICE COUNCIL, THE DUTIES OF THE POLICE COUNCIL ARE:

ELECTED

POLICE COMMISSIONERS: SEVEN
ONE COMMISSIONER FOR EACH NEIGHBORHOOD DIVISION,
THE DUTIES OF THE COMMISSIONERS ARE:

QUALIFICATIONS FOR POLICE COUNCILMEN:

1. RESIDENCE IN HIS PRECINCT FOR SIX MONTHS PRIOR TO THE U—
   COMING ELECTION,
2. MUST BE OF VOTING AGE,

DUTIES OF POLICE COUNCILMEN:

1. SET QUALIFICATIONS FOR SELECTION OF POLICEMEN,
2. HEAR AND ACT ON COMPLAINTS OF PEOPLE AGAINST
   POLICEMEN,
3. DISCIPLINE POLICEMEN WHO BREAK LAWS OR POLICIES
   WITHIN THE DISTRICT,
4. SELECT ONE COMMISSIONER TO REPRESENT THE PEOPLE
   ON THE BOARD OF COMMISSIONERS, THEY CAN FIRE HIM,
   TOO, IF THEY'RE NOT SATISFIED WITH HIS ACTIONS,
5. MAKE POLICY DECISIONS, THE COMMISSIONER FOR THAT
   POLICE COUNCIL IS BOUND TO BRING UP THESE DECISIONS
   AT COMMISSIONERS' MEETINGS AND VOTE ACCORDING TO
   THE POLICE COUNCILS INSTRUCTIONS,

THE POLICE COMMISSIONERS FORM THE POLICE COM—
MISSION, FOR EACH POLICE DEPARTMENT IN THE CITY,

DUTIES OF POLICE COMMISSIONERS:

1. SELECT POLICEMEN,
2. DISCIPLINE POLICEMEN,
3. SET QUALIFICATIONS FOR POLICEMEN,
4. SET POLICIES WITHIN THE POLICE DEPARTMENT,
5. FIX SALARIES OF POLICE COUNCILMEN AND POLICEMEN,
6. MAKE NECESSARY AGREEMENTS WITH OTHER POLICE
   DEPARTMENTS AND GOVERNMENT AGENCIES,

COMMUNITY CONTROL OF POLICE MEANS

CONTROL OF OUR DESTINIES: SELF DETERMINATION FOR ALL PEOPLES,

AN END TO THE RACIST HARRASSMENT BY POLICE, HUEY NEWTON,
BOBBY SEALE, LOS SIETE AND MANY OTHER POLITICAL PRISONERS WOULD NOT BE
IN JAIL TODAY IF WE HAD COMMUNITY CONTROL OF POLICE,

POLICE COULD NOT BE USED AS STRIKE BREAKERS BY THE
RULING CLASS, BECAUSE IF THEY DO NOT REPRESENT THE INTEREST OF
THE PEOPLE THEY WILL BE EXPELLED FROM THE DEPARTMENT,

FULLER EMPLOYMENT IN LOW INCOME COMMUNITIES BECAUSE
RESIDENTS OF THE COMMUNITY WOULD BE EMPLOYED AS POLICEMEN,

POWER TO THE PEOPLE

POWER TO THE PEOPLE!

THE ACTION BEGINS WITH EACH POLICE COUNCIL PRECINCT—(A 6—TO 10 BLOCK ARE
BLOCK AREA, PRECINCT VOTERS ELECT ONE COUNCILMAN WHO MUST LIVE IN
THAT AREA, THIS COUNCILMAN IS ONE OF IS ON THE POLICE COUNCIL OF EACH
NEIGHBORHOOD DIVISION:

POLICE DEPARTMENT #1: BLACK WORKING CLASS COMMUNITY
7 NEIGHBORHOOD DIVISIONS

POLICE DEPARTMENT #2: BROWN WORKING CLASS COMMUNITY
5 NEIGHBORHOOD DIVISIONS

POLICE DEPARTMENT #3: CHINESE WORKING CLASS COMMUNITY
2 NEIGHBORHOOD DIVISIONS

POLICE DEPARTMENT #4: WHITE WORKING CLASS COMMUNITY
7 NEIGHBORHOOD DIVISIONS

POLICE DEPARTMENT #5: RULING CLASS COMMUNITY:
3 NEIGHBORHOOD DIVISIONS

EACH POLICE DEPT, LOOKS LIKE THIS:

THE PEOPLE OF EACH PRECINCT ELECT ONE COUNCILMAN

POLICE COUNCIL FOR ONE NEIGHBORHOOD DIVISION (IS:COUNCILMEN)

7 POLICE COMMISSIONERS

THE POWER IS RETURNED TO THE PEOPLE

THIS IS A REVOLUTIONARY PROGRAM:

THE COMMUNITY CONTROL OF POLICE PETITION PROVIDES THAT ALL
WEAPONS, VEHICLES, EQUIPMENT, FUNDS AND FILES OF THE PRESENT
FASCIST POLICE FORCE WILL BE DISTRIBUTED TO THE PEOPLE'S COM—
MUNITY POLICE DEPARTMENTS . (Section 35,1—A of petition)

POLICE BECOME COMMUNITY PEOPLE
ALL POLICE OFFICERS MUST LIVE IN THE POLICE DEPARTMENT AREAS
THEY WORK IN, (Section 35,1—B)

THE YOUTH HAVE A STRONG VOICE

COUNCILMEN CAN BE RECALLED BY A PETITION BEARING THE SIGNATURES
OF RESIDENTS EQUALLING 20% OF THE NUMBER OF PEOPLE VOTING IN THAT PRE—
CINCT, THE 20% SIGNING DO NOT HAVE TO BE REGISTERED VOTERS AND THEY
CAN BE OF ANY AGE,
COMMISSIONERS CAN BE RECALLED (through a petition) BY 20% OF THE REGIS—
TERED VOTERS IN THAT PRECINCT.

ary changes. They concentrate their efforts and support at strategic relevant points such as their own working places and those of dependent labor, the counter-institutions, the oppressed communities, the black ghettos, the prisons and the third world countries.

In cooperation with the different politically organized liberation movements in communities, factories and prisons, planners especially can work within the oppressed communities where grass-roots radical organizations are mobilizing people around their daily problems and frustrations. They can work theoretically and practically on problems for self-organization, self-determination, self-defense and collective liberation. While local radical community power increases, interventions from the outside, including all kinds of aggressive physical and societal system interferences, meet more and more effective resistance.

Where advice and support are needed, they can practice both their future role as organizer of a revolutionary society and environment and their present role as societal and urban guerilla. They can also work on practical small-scale revolutionary strategies and theoretical large-scale strategies.

Within this political framework, the human solution of *small-scale* urban problems becomes more realizable. Only then can planners develop new planning approaches which are truly based on cooperation with the people concerned. These are not only new models of participation but also urban models which can be based on effective participation and *collective planning systems approaches:* models which can generate concurrent structures of social, economic and political urban functions, which integrate all organizational, social educational facilities, residential areas of the past and the future. Actual solutions for large-scale urban problems, however, can only be prepared theoretically, since within the present political conditions of America there is no chance at this time for practical feedback.

In such situations, the reorganization of the given political and economic structure according to socialist values seems to be the only real chance of implementing *large-scale human-oriented urban solutions* and of stopping further "urban massacres."

As revolutionary movement and organizations are permanently threatened to become destroyed by the System's brutality (compare the prosecution of leaders and members of the Black Panther Party) and as their ideological concepts still deviate too much from each other, a united front against the system seems practically and theoretically to be premature.

At this point the incremental approach of the radical situational groups, however — one community, one prison, one radicalized cell at a time in action — seems tactically to be appropriate to safeguard the continuation of revolutionary theory and action until time for a united front will come.

I MET BOLIVAR ON A
LONG MORNING...
"FATHER," I SAID, "ARE YOU,
OR ARE YOU NOT, OR
WHO ARE YOU?"
AND HE SAID:

"I RISE EVERY
HUNDRED YEARS
WHEN THE PEOPLE
WAKE UP."
—PABLO NERUDA

FOOTNOTES

CHAPTER I

1. Cf. Herbert Marcuse, "The End of Utopia," *Five Lectures* (Boston: Beacon Press, 1970), pp. 62-84. Reprinted in *Ramparts,* (April, 1970).

2. "Social reproduction" refers to those components which maintain and reproduce a society as a whole, such as its political structure, institutionalization, organization of production means and the basic personality of its individuals.

3. We refer to the best-known utopian socialists in the beginning of the nineteenth century: e.g. Fourier, Owens, Cabot et al.

4. Cf. Marcuse, *op. cit.*

5. Technical rationality can be defined as partial rationality which is reduced to pure technical form. In our society it has become an instrument of disposed power and technified domination. Cf. Herbert Marcuse, *One-Dimensional Man* (Boston: Beacon Press, 1968), pp. 1-19.

6. "If utopia wants to theoretically conceive the practical necessity of its dissolution (or implementation) derived from the experiences of existing contradictions, then it must scientifically legitimize its cognitive interests in a doubled way: namely, as an actual objective need and as an objective possible realization." Jürgen Habermas, *Theorie und Praxis* (Frankfurt: Suhrkamp, 1963), p. 350.

7. Cf. Robert Boguslaw, *The New Utopians: A Study of Systems Research and Social Change* (New York: Prentice-Hall, Inc., 1965).

8. Marcuse, *op. cit.*

CHAPTER II

1. "Society is on the one hand full of contradictions and on the other hand it can be determined. It is rational and irrational in one, system and disintegration, blind nature, but still mediated through consciousness . . . Without the anticipation of structural fact — the totality, which can hardly be adequately understood in its individual parts — no individual observation could be judged . . . The social totality, however, has no self-dynamic outside of the synthesis from which it has been formed. It produces and reproduces itself through individual components. Many of these possess a relative independence, of which primitive but total societies are either unaware or intolerant. Just as little as the totality can be separated from life, even so little can any one elemental part be understood only in terms of its functioning without reflections in the whole, which has the movement of each elemental part as its essence." Theodor Adorno, "Logik der Socialwissenschaften," *Kölner Zeitschrift für Soziologie und Sozialpsychologie* (Vol. 14, 1962).

2. Lloyd A. Free and Hadley Cantril describe *"Liberalism old-style"* as similar to the classical concept of *laissez-faire. "Liberalism new-style"* on the other hand, refers to the program for social reform and the redistribution of resources towards a welfare state, proposed by the "liberals." They are in opposition to the conservatives, who still believe in a *laissez-faire* state within the framework of "law and order." Cf. Lloyd A. Free and Hadley Cantril, *The Political Beliefs of Americans* (New Brunswick, N.J.: Rutgers University Press, 1967).

3. Dirigism stands for centralized and planned state interventions which renounce direct and critical citizen feedback.

4. Like the Keynesian theories or Franklin D. Roosevelt's New Deal programs.

5. "Thus the New Deal was essentially a political response (not economic) to the great depression and a brilliantly successful strategy to save capitalism." Actual economic solutions came finally through World War II. M. E. Gettelman and David Mermelstein, *The Great Society Reader* (New York, N. Y.: Vintage Books, 1967), p. 45.

6. The concept of rationalization was introduced by Max Weber. It includes the rational organization of technologies and the correct choice of given alternatives. Jürgen Habermas describes both of these as types of *purposive-rational action* (that is, rational with regard only to purposes or ends). Then planning is used to establish, to improve and to enlarge an effective system of all kinds of *purposive-rational* actions. Marcuse is convinced that what Weber calls rationalization realizes not *rationality as such* but rather, in the name of rationality, a specific form of unacknowledged political domination. Because this sort of rationality extends to the correct choice among strategies, the appropriate application of technologies and the efficient establishment of systems (with presupposed aims in given situations) it removes the *total social framework of interests* in which strategies are chosen, technologies applied and systems established from the scope of *reflection* and *rational reconstruc-*

tion. Marcuse concludes: "the very concept of technical reason is perhaps ideological. Not only the application of technology but technology itself is domination (of nature and men) methodical, scientific, calculated, calculating control . . . Technology is always a historical-social project: in it is projected what a society and its ruling interests intend to do with men and things. Such a 'purpose' of domination is 'substantive' and to this extent belongs to the very form of technological reason." Jürgen Habermas, *Toward A Rational Society* (Boston: Beacon Press, 1970), p. 82.

7. Tom Hayden, "Welfare Liberalism and Social Change," *The Great Society Reader,* p. 477.

8. Liberalism new-style concerns the twentieth century liberals' programs as opposed to the conservatives'.

9. *The Man's Technology,* SDS paper given to the Conference on "Conversion," (Cambridge, 1969), p. 3.

10. As a result of the current ideologies the welfare-state is identified with "more human society." The analysis of the present America or of fascism in pre-war Italy and Germany and present Greece and Spain shows that welfare itself can easily be integrated into inhuman political systems.

11. Hayden, *op. cit.,* p. 477.

12. An example is the housing situation in America. Poor people desperately need decent housing. But their demand is ineffective — i.e. they can't afford the high rents for the profit-interested housing-producer and owner — their vital need is simply ignored by the housing industry and authorities.

13. Christoph Feldkeller, "Theorie und Praxis," Journal *Arch.* + (July, 1969), p. 8.

14. Both the companies of Penn Central Inc., and Lockheed after their bankrupcies in 1970 received enormous government extra support to overcome their crises.

15. See Isard and Karaska, *Unclassified Defense and Space Contracts; Awards by County, State and Metropolitan Area, United States,* Fiscal year 1964, p. 2. and Claus Offe, "Unemployment of Scientists and Engineers," Journal of *Science for People* (December, 1970), p. 5.

16. See Footnote 6.

17. Andrew Hacker, *The Man's Technology,* p. 3.

18. Cf. Jacques Ellul, *The Technological So-*

ciety (New York: Alfred A. Knopf Company, 1964); and the works of Max Weber.

19. Cf. R. D. Laing, *The Divided Self* (Harmondsworth: Penguin Books, 1965).

CHAPTER III

1. Shadrach Woods, *What Can U Do?* Architecture at Rice 27 (Rice University, 1970), p. 5.

2. "Today any form of transformation of the technical and natural environment is a possibility . . . " "All the material and intellectual forces which could be put to work for the realization of a free society are at hand." Herbert Marcuse, *Five Lectures,* p. 64.

3. New York City, for example, pays $3 billion to Albany and $15 billion to Washington in yearly taxes, from which a total of only $2½ billion returns to the City. See: Nixon's "open housing" bill prohibiting subsidized housing in suburbs.

4. Seventy-three per cent of all Americans live in cities of more than 2,500 inhabitants.

5. Cf. Hans Harms, *User Involvement in Housing and Planning,* unpublished paper presented at the AAAS Conference (Boston, 1970).

6. Compare the institutionalized forms of planning in European or socialist countries.

7. Cf. "Technocracy and Technocratic Planning," Chapter III.

8. Cf. Charles E. Lindbloom, "The Science of Muddling Through," *Public Administration Review* (Vol. 19, 1959).

9. "Planning-for-the-whole" means comprehensive planning combined with all available social data.

10. Compare New York City's latest so-called "comprehensive plan" (MIT Press) and its critiques (New York Review of Books). The plan in its essence is a simple reflection of present business interests.

11. Cf. "Participatory Planning vs. System Approaches," Chapter VII.

12. Cf. Peter Marris and Martin Rein, *Dilemmas of Social Reform, Poverty and Community Action in the U.S.* (New York: Atherton Press, 1967).

13. Cf. Fred Powledge, *Model City* (New York: Simon & Schuster, 1970).

14. Cf. Daniel P. Moynihan, "The Professionalization of Reform," *The Great Society Reader,* p. 456.

15. a) Claus Offe says about institutions: "Several sociological and scientific politi-

cal analyses, studying the existent institutions (political parties, parliaments, mass medias, organizations) found out that the institutions of the political system are increasingly sealed up by tendencies to bureaucratism and power concentrations against the possibility of becoming instruments of public articulation of interests . . . Structural imperatives and structural absolutism are not necessary structural elements developed in industrial societies, but are the consequence of an institutional defect. Structural imperatives rule where the institutions of the public are dried out or where it has failed to replace them by new political institutions."
Claus Offe, "Sachzwang und Entscheidungspielraum," Journal *Bauwelt* (September, 1969).

b) From a similar position, Marcuse demands the establishment of a "direct democracy" and the abolition of the indirect one which is misused as an institution for the perpetuation of the ruling elites through votes and representation. Cf. Herbert Marcuse, *One-Dimensional Man.*

c) Habermas, speaking for the radicalization of the middle classes, within the framework of liberal democracy, argues for the sublimation of the representative democracy through participation and the generation of a critical public. Goals should be the emancipation and liberation of the individual from the present oppressive ruling conditions through public communication, institutionally affirmed use of "liberated" spaces and places, and human-related, publicly-controlled use of new technologies. Cf. Jürgen Habermas, *Theorie und Praxis.*

d) Huey Newton speaks for those most oppressed by the present institutions, calling for a socialist government to bring about equality and a new constitution so that everyone will enjoy the same rights and privileges. Huey Newton, quoted in *Boston Globe* (August, 1970).

16. "Ombudsman" is a government official who investigates citizen complaints against government agencies — a Swedish innovation from 1809.

17. Chandler H. Stevens, "Citizen Feedback: The Need and The Response," *Technological Review* (January, 1971), p. 43.

18. Claus Offe, "Sachzwang und Entscheidungspielraum."

19. C. West Churchman, "Architecture and Operational Research," *Architectural Design* (September, 1969), p. 487.

20. Alex Tzonis, "The Last Identity Crisis in Architecture," *Connection* (Spring, 1969).

CHAPTER IV

1. A system is "a composition, an addition, an ordered whole, an arrangement of parts into the whole. The whole is complete within itself, and not merely a collection of parts." Siegfried Maser, "Systemtheorie," Journal *Arch.* + 2 (April, 1968), p. 21.

2. System classification in applied systems theory, still very new, is continually changing according to advancing research. We will therefore decline to give an overview here.

3. Cf. Robin Evans, "The Social History of Artifact Systems," *Architectural Association Quarterly* (January, 1970).

4. Warren Brodey, "Soft Architecture," Journal *Landscape* (Autumn, 1967).

5. Richard J. Barnet, Journal *Der Spiegel* (No. 1/2,1970).

6. Cf. Buckminster Fuller, Edwin Schlossberg and Daniel Gildesgane, *The World Game Report* (NYC: New York Studio School, 1969).

7. Cf. Jay W. Forrester, *World Dynamics* (Cambridge: Wright Allen Press, 1971).

8. Jay W. Forrester in "Counterintuitive Behavior of Social Systems," Journal *Technology Review* (January, 1971), p. 67.

9. Journal *Der Spiegel, loc. cit.*

10. Cf. Jay W. Forrester, *Urban Dynamics* (Cambridge: MIT Press, 1969).

11. Cf. Walter Buckley, *Sociology and Modern Systems Theory* (Englewood Cliffs, N.J.: Prentice-Hall, Inc., 1967).

12. Organic Model	Mechanical Model
flexible, less organization	inflexible, highly organized
high entropy	low entropy
no normative behavior	normative behavior
unpredictable	predictable
self-given constraint	outside constraints
responsive to environments	unresponsive to environments

Whereby high entropy (low negentropy) means the tendency to greater order and organization, and low entropy (high negentropy) means toward greater randomness and disorder. C. Abel and W. R. Ashby, "Urban Chaos or Self-Organization?" Journal *Architectural Design* (September, 1969), pp. 501-502.

13. See Footnote 12.

14. Feedback processes are goal-seeking (negative feedback structures), or learning and growing processes (positive feedback).

15. Alexeij Gutnov, *The Ideal Communist City* (N.Y. Braziller, i press, 1970), p. 21.

16. "System" is used for U.S. capitalism as a total system.

17. Alex Tzonis, "The Last Identity Crisis of Architecture" *Connection*.

18. Compare the city of West Berlin, one of the few present-day cities that actually does have closed functional and formal boundaries. Her survival depends mostly on outside support, enormous tax reduction and propaganda to attract new inhabitants.

19. Cf. Melvin Webber, "Roles of Intelligence Systems in Urban-Systems Planning," *Journal AIP* (November, 1965).

CHAPTER V

1. "A collection of sets forms a semi-lattice if, and only if, when two overlapping sets belong to the collection, then the set of elements common to both also belongs to the collection." Christopher Alexander, "A City is Not a Tree," Journal *Design* (Vol. 206, 1966), p. 47.

2. "A collection of sets forms a tree if and only if for any two sets that belong to the collection either one is wholly contained in the other or else they are wholly disjoined." *Ibid.*

3. Edward Banfield, quoted by C. Alexander, *op. cit.*

4. Cf. Nicholaus Luhman, *Zweckbegriff und Systemrationalität* (Tübingen: C. B. Mohr, 1969).

5. Concepts have recently been developed for this within decision theory and heuristic modelling.

6. Richard J. Dietrich, "Metastadt," Journal *Deutsche Bauzeitung* (January, 1969).

CHAPTER VI

1. Cf. Robert Boguslaw, *The New Utopians.*

2. Cf. Ira S. Lowry, "A Short Course in Model Design," Journal *AIP* (May, 1968).

3. Cf. Chapter IV, Footnote 14.

4. "Social feedforward," means to acquire knowledge and information both forward from the center of society to the citizens and forward in time so as to suggest what consequences will likely occur if various choices

are made by individual citizens and by the society as a whole. Cf. Chandler H. Stevens, "Citizen Feedback: The Need and the Response."

5. Maurice Kilbridge, Robert O'Block and Paul Teplitz, "The Role of Models in Urban Planning," Journal *Arch. +* (Vol. 2, 1969).

6. See table number 6 and Cf. C. West Churchman, *The Systems Approach* (NYC: Delta Books, 1968) and Lowry, *op. cit.*

7. Kilbridge *et al, op. cit.*, p. 35.

8. Comparatively, Marcuse says about labor in capitalism: ". . . the only thing that can happen within it is for labor to be organized as rationally as possible and reduced as much as possible. But it remains labor in and of the realm of necessity and thereby unfree." Herbert Marcuse, *Five Lectures,* p. 28.

9. Cf. David R. Seidman, *The Construction of an Urban Growth Model* (Philadelphia: Delaware Valley Regional Planning Commission, 1969), p. 262.

10. Cf. James Hester, Jr., "Systems Models of Urban Growth and Development" (Cambridge: MIT Urban Systems Lab, 1969).

11. "We know that he (the human designer) must interpret human needs and desires but we do not know how to describe these needs and desires." Nicolaus Negroponte, Journal *Architectural Design* (September, 1969), p. 511.

12. We argue that what is describable is programmable and we argue the converse of the contrapositive as well: that what is not describable is not programmable." A statement from the MIT Urban Systems Laboratory, Journal *Architectural Design* (September, 1969), p. 510.

13. David R. Seidman, *op. cit.,* p.263.

14. Cf. Maurice Kilbridge and Jon Didrichsen, "Abstraction, Verification and Validation in Urban Simulation," Journal *Arch. +* (Vol. 8, 1969).

15. Robert Boguslaw, *op. cit.*

16. *Ibid.*

17. Ira S. Lowry, *A Model of Metropolis* (Rand Corporation, Santa Monica, 1964), p. 5.

18. Ira S. Lowry, *A Short Course in Model Design* (Santa Monica: Rand Corp., 1965) quoting Nathaniel Lichtfeld in "Cost Benefit Analysis in City Planning," *Journal AIP* (Vol. 26, November, 1960), pp. 273-279.

19. Ira S. Lowry, *Seven Models of Urban Environment* (Santa Monica: Rand Corporation, 1967), p. 5.

20. Cf. Jay W. Forrester, *Urban Dynamics* (Cambridge: MIT Press, 1969).
21. Cf. Jay W. Forrester, *Industrial Dynamics* (Cambridge: MIT Press, 1961).
22. Forrester, *Urban Dynamics,* p. 109.
23. *Ibid.,* pp. 2, 17.
24. *Ibid.,* p. 15.
25. *Ibid.,* p. 71.
26. *Ibid.*
27. Kilbridge *et al,* "The Role of Models in Urban Planning," p. 41.

CHAPTER VII

1. *The Man's Technology* (Cf. Chapter II, Footnote 9), p. 6.
2. Richard J. Dietrich, "Metastadt."
3. Cf. Nicolaus Negroponte, *The Architecture Machine* (Cambridge: MIT Press, 1970), and "Towards a Humanism Through Machines," Journal *Architectural Design,* Sept., 1969.
4. Nicolaus Negroponte in *Architectural Design.*
5. Richard Hessdorfer in "Interact" *Architectural Design.*
6. Cf. Chandler H. Stevens, "Citizen Feedback," and Thomas B. Sheridan in "Citizen Feedback: New Technology for Social Choice," *Technological Review.*
7. "Involvement of the right people during the design and construction of an applied model can determine ultimate success or failure of the project. Who are the right people? Those directly responsible for the planning efforts in which the model will be used — the professionals of the planning department, certain policy makers, elected and appointed public officials, the managers of some municipal departments. These people must understand the general theory of the model if their decisions are to be aided by it." (Sic!). Maurice Kilbridge, p. 124.
8. *The Man's Technology, loc. cit.,* p. 5.
9. *The Cambridge Project* (SDS pamphlet, 1969).
10. *Ibid.,* p. 42.
11. *Ibid.*
12. Eberhard Schnelle, "Entscheidung und Planung," Journal *Arch.* + (Vol. 2, 1968).
13. Paul Baran and Paul M. Sweezy, *Monopoly Capital* (New York City: Modern Reader Paperbacks, 1968), p. 42.
14. "The Waitress," a guideline to Valle's Steak House.
15. Martin Oppenheimer, *The Urban Guerilla* (Chicago: Quadrangle Books, 1969), p. 24.

CHAPTER VIII

1. "For among a great part of the manipulated population in the developed capitalist countries the need for freedom does no longer exist as a vital, necessary need.

"It is precisely the continuity of needs developed and satisfied in a repressive society that reproduces this repressive society over and over again within the individuals themselves.

"Individuals reproduce society in their needs which persist even through revolution and it is precisely this continuity which up to now has stood in the way of the leap from quantity into the quality of free society." Herbert Marcuse, *Five Lectures,* p. 30.
2. Claus Offe, "Sachzwang und Entscheidungsspielraum."
3. See Chapter III, "Pragmatic Planning."
4. Cf. Nicolaus Negroponte, *The Architecture Machine.*
5. Compare the new self-determining decentralist collective planning approaches in China which generate a new kind of industrial revolution. Most products relate directly to the people's needs and their specific situations.
6. Paul Davidoff, "Advocacy and Pluralism in Planning," *AIP Journal* (Vol. 4, 1968) and "A Choice Theory of Planning," *AIP Journal* (Vol. 3, 1969).
7. Edmund M. Burke, "Citizen Participation Strategies," *AIP Journal* (September, 1968).
8. Cf. Edward Banfield, *The Heavenly City* (Boston: Little Brown, 1970).
9. Richard Senett, "Survival for the Fattest," *New York Review of Books* (August, 1970), p. 23.
10. Cf. Banfield, *op. cit.*
11. Senett, *op. cit.*
12. The following steps mark the formative stages of personality:

    1) relationship of mother and infant; a stage in which the genotype or hereditary features unfold and in which the foundations are laid for social thresholds of perception.

    2) relationship with parents, a stage at which different social relationships begin to be distinguished and language is formed.

    3) relationships with other children.

    4) preliminary self-determination of the personality: relationships arise in the process of learning. Cognitive norms are be-

ing assimilated and personal attitudes are being formed through differentiation among social relationships.

5) economic relationships; a stage permitting the individual to validate his attitudes in a working environment and to establish his personal identity.

6) relationships that give a person social value through activities freely initiated by him and through his participation in the cultural life of his time.

7) relationships arising out of consumer activities.

8) sexual relationships that serve to continue the generational process.

It is important to note that each stage can be defined in terms of its characteristic social relationships. Alexeij Gutnov, *op. cit.*

i press series on the human environment